The Awesome All's

The Awesome All's

LEHMAN STRAUSS

AMBASSADOR

BELFAST ◆ GREENVILLE
NORTHERN IRELAND ◆ SOUTH CAROLINA

The Awesome All's
Copyright © 1998 Lehman Strauss

ISBN 1 84030 022 1

Ambassador Publications
a division of
Ambassador Productions Ltd.
Providence House
16 Hillview Avenue,
Belfast, BT5 6JR
Northern Ireland

Emerald House
1 Chick Springs Road, Suite 206
Greenville,
South Carolina 29609, USA

Contents

———————— ❖ ————————

❖❖❖

Foreword

❖

What a great pleasure it was for us to have Dr. Lehman Strauss in the Iron Hall Assembly in September of 1996.

Having heard a lot about Dr. Strauss, and having read many of his books we looked forward to his visit to Ulster with anticipation. We were not disappointed. His biblical insight, his timely application, his gracious and simple delivery, and also his warm personality shone through time and again. The series he took for the week was entitled, **"The Alls of Scripture".** Night after night, preaching to eager congregations Dr. Strauss warmed our hearts. Our experience was like the two on the road to Emmaus, we could say, "Did not our hearts burn within us, while he talked with us by the way, and while He opened to us the Scriptures."

Dr. Strauss and his wife, Diane, planned to be with us again in the autumn of this year, but God had other plans. We were saddened to hear of his home-call to glory some time ago and yet through this new book, "he being dead yet speaketh".

I commend this new book to you and trust that through it the Saviour, whom Lehman loved, will be glorified, God's people will be refreshed and sinners will be drawn to the Cross.

Pastor Denis Lyle
Lurgan Baptist Church
Spring 1998

The All of Scripture

--- ❖ ---

Open your Bible please to Paul's second epistle to Timothy chapter 3 verse 16. The first word in that verse is the key to our studies. They all have to do with the most inclusive word in any language, it is the word A-L-L - All. In this study we will deal with the All of the Scriptures. Later in this series we will reflect on the All of Sin. That is very unpopular, people don't want to hear the subject of sin. Someone wrote a book recently in America called *Whatever Became of Sin?*

But now, the All of the Scriptures, verse 16 please. "All scripture." Interpreted from the original text every writing, every inscriptured word is given by inspiration of God. Not some of it, not much of it, not most of it - all of it. I was saddened when a friend of many years contacted me to say he was rethinking the Scriptures, saying that he was not sure that all of it is the Word of God but that he believes it contains the Word of God. Sorry folks, it does not merely contain the Word of God, it is all the Word of God. All Scripture is given by inspiration of God and is profitable. *Notice that for which it is profitable.*

First of all for doctrine. Now the word doctrine means teaching. Therefore the Scriptures are given to teach us what is right. Right doctrine will be found within the confines of God's Book. Not all doctrine is right. The right doctrine is in the Word. So it is profitable for doctrine - what is right. *It is profitable for reproof* - what is not right.

I have been wrong through my 60 years in the ministry more than once and I have always been grateful and thankful to God for someone along the way who has helped me to see where I was in error. Your Pastor was mentioning my commentary on Revelation. I did not know Pastor, whether you noted that in the front of that book it says copyright. I should tell you what that means. That means copy right out of it.

I could rewrite that book. I would not change my doctrinal position. I could rewrite it because I have studied. I wrote that book, I guess, 40 years ago. I would not change my doctrine but I picked up truth along the way and sometimes I needed to be reproved. Someone has to say that is not right and I thank them for that. It is profitable for doctrine what is right, for reproof what is not right and *for correction how to get right.* If we are not right in our doctrine we come to the Bible and we will discover how to get right. The Bible is God's inspired, inerrant, infallible, immutable, indestructible Word. If you want to get right you come to the Book. It is where you get right.

Then it is also profitable for instruction how to stay right. If I am not right I want to get right. I want to be reproved, I want to correct my errors and then I want to stay right. So we are introduced to the first All in our study and that is the All of Scripture.

Now turn to the epistle to the Hebrews and look at chapter four. I am going to do something that I have taught my students not to do. I have taught them that you do not add anything to the Word of God or you don't take anything from the Word of God and you don't change anything in the Word of God. That is a good base from which to open your Bible and read and study. But I have added a word, no I have added a letter to a word. Hebrews 4:12. On the basis of II Timothy 3:16 every Scripture, every written word that God gave, it all came from Him and it is profitable. Therefore I read Hebrews 4:12 like this - For the words of God are quick, living, life producing, life preserving - because God's words, they are living words. They are powerful, energising and they are penetrating, they are sharper than any two-edged sword, piercing even to the dividing asunder of souls and spirit, and of the joints and marrow, and is a discerner of the thoughts and intents of the hearts. Is not that a great text which describes the Word of God. Living, energising.

So, for a little while, we would like to listen to God speak. May I say, dear friends, we better listen up because God is going to say something and just as surely as we are in this meeting what He says must come to pass. If it does not we are in the wrong place, we are working with the wrong book, we are worshipping the wrong God. God's words are living, life producing, life preserving.

Now for a little while we will look at three areas where we will hear God speak and let us see how powerful, how energising His words are.

Let us go back to page one, that is a good place to begin in your Bible. Turn to Genesis chapter 1. The Bible opens with these words "In the Beginning God created the heaven and the earth." Did you ever wonder how He did it? Now there are some folks today who tell us that all that we know about came into existence by an evolutionary process. Don't believe that dear friends, there is not any evolution in the Bible. Absolutely not. In the beginning God created the heaven and the earth and He did not do it by evolutionary process.

Many years ago I had to study a text book on biology with the Darwinian theory of evolution that we came from animals and I had the opportunity to speak to the professor who taught that. I said, "Dear sir, some of your ancestors might have hung by their necks but none ever hung by their tails, that's for sure." In the beginning God created. Now the word "create" appears three times in Genesis 1. Verse 1, the physical universe. All world stuff and physical matter. The second appearance is in verse 21 with animal life. Now you don't have to be a university graduate to understand that that which you have in verse 21 did not evolve from that which you have in verse 1. In verse 21 that is a separate and distinct act of creation on a separate and distinct occasion. There is no evolution between verse1 and verse 21. Then the next time you have the word create it is in verse 27 - *so God created man*. It is a distinct act of creation on a distinct and separate occasion. There is no evolution between verse 21 and verse 27. How did God do it?

The first recorded words of God are in Genesis 1:3. If you mark your Bible you might want to underline these three words "And God said". Now God is going to say something. We better listen up because if what God says does not come to pass we have got the wrong book and we have got the wrong God. What are the first recorded words of

God? "And God said," now listen up, "Let there be light:" and what are the next four words in your Bible "and there was light". Why was there light? Because God said so. Is not that so simple. God spoke light into being. "God said". Suppose you and I could have been there when God said "let there be light" and we heard Him say it. What would we expect? Now if we did not know God we would not know what to expect. But if we knew the God who uttered the words we would know that we would expect to see light. Why? Because God said so.

Now move down the page just a little bit to verse 6 "And God said". Now you can read verses six and seven but look at the last four words in verse 7 "and it was so". Why was it so? Because God said so. Now that is so plain in your Bible you cannot pass it up. Look at verse 9 "And God said" read what He said and read the last four words of verse 9 "and it was so". Why was it so? Because God said so. The words of God are living, operative, energising. When God speaks something happens, "for all Scripture is given by inspiration of God." Verse 11 "And God said" read the verse, "and it was so". Verse 14 "And God said" the last four words in verse 15 "and it was so". Verse 20 "And God said" every time God spoke what God said came to pass. That is the book all about a man. The man is the Lord Jesus Christ and the book is the Bible, the Word of God. God speaks through His Word.

Now what we have here dear friends is a natural creation. A natural creation. You say, "Do you really believe that God spoke it into being?" Turn to Psalm 33 there is a verse or two there which I would like you to see. Psalm 33: 6. Now the Psalmist is reiterating what Moses wrote in Genesis, "By the word of the Lord were the heavens made; and all the host of them by the breath of his mouth." That is saying what Moses wrote in Genesis chapter one. Look at verse 9 "For he spake, and it was done, he commanded, and it stood fast." Does that not warm the cockles of your heart and make you feel good about your Bible? When God speaks something happens. We better listen up when we are reading this book for God has something to say to us.

Now what God controls. You read within the confines of this book not less than five times these words or similar to them "heaven and earth will pass away but My words shall never pass away" God's immutable, indestructible Word, what God creates God controls. The Bible will stand. We used to sing an old chorus, *The Bible Stands,* do you sing that here in Ireland? It is a great song! I should teach it to you.

Now we have a natural creation. Turn with me please to another chapter in the book of Genesis, chapter 12. What is the first creation that God spoke into being? The natural world, the natural creation, the universe, the physical universe. Now look at Genesis 12:1 "Now the Lord had said," now you have to listen up again because God is going to say something and if what He says does not come to pass forget Him and forget this Book. It would be nice to pronounce the final benediction, dismiss the meeting and never open the doors again if it does not come to pass. If you cannot trust God why come and go through the ritual of worship. If I can't trust it why bother? God is going to say something now. "Now the Lord had said unto Abram, Get thee out of thy country, and from thy kindred and from thy father's house unto a land that I will shew thee." Now notice the "I wills", God is speaking and we have to listen up. "I will make of thee a great nation, and I will bless thee, and make thy name great and thou shalt be a blessing: And I will bless them that bless thee, and curse him that curseth thee: and in these shall all families of the earth be blessed."

Dear friends, my wife's background and mine are different. Her ancestors came from Scotland and I am a Jew by birth. My father was a German who came from Germany to the United States. Now when you get a Scotswoman and a Jew married together you have got some ancient controversy to get over. When we were in Scotland, Diane and I learned an awful lot of things about Scotland and the Scots people. Since she has been married to me she has picked up a few ideas about the Jewish people. Now let me say this, the Jewish nation is God's creation. Now you have a natural creation by the Word of God and you have *a national creation by the Word of God.* In every generation from Isaac to Jesus Christ, a male child had to be born to preserve the line until the Messiah would come. I can say this: Any orthodox Jew who has studied the Old Testament ought to know that Jesus Christ is the promised Messiah.

He was born from the right family genealogically, David. He was born in the right place geographically, (Micah 5:2), Bethlehem. He was born in the right manner biologically, (Isaiah 7:14), a virgin shall conceive. He was born at the right time chronologically, (Galatians 4:4), "When the fullness of the time was come God sent forth His Son." I say every orthodox Jew ought to know from his Old Testament that Jesus Christ is the promised Messiah. Now that nation will never be wiped off the face of the earth. Your Bible is before you. Turn to the prophecy of Jeremiah at chapter 31. I would like you to see something in your Bible because God is going to say something and we should look carefully because this is important. Every major country in the world with possibly one or two exceptions has tried to wipe out the nation of Israel. One thing that the nations have been after is the inestimable wealth of the Dead Sea. Just to get the minerals out of the Dead Sea would provide enough money to any nation to keep them out of debt. They are after the wealth of the Dead Sea and they would like to get everything away from Israel. Jeremiah 31:35 "Thus saith the Lord," now listen up because He is going to say something. Is it important?   Everything God says is important. There is no fooling around when God speaks dear friends. "Thus saith the Lord, which giveth the sun for a light by day, and the ordinances of the moon and of the stars for a light by night, which divideth the sea when the waves thereof roar: The Lord of hosts is His name." Now this is what He is going to say, "If those ordinances depart from before Me, saith the Lord, then the seed of Israel also shall cease from being a nation before Me for ever." Anybody like to try for it? Would you like to wipe out the nation of Israel? You have got to destroy the sun, moon and stars first. Who said so? God said so. And along with the promise of the Messiah is the promise of the land, that geographical location that God gave to Israel. A national creation and what God creates God controls.

Let's look at a third creation. Turn with me now to II Corinthians 5:17 "Therefore if any man be in Christ, he is a new creature." Now we have a natural creation by the words of God we have a national creation by the words of God. Now we have a new creation. What is this new creation? It is a remarkable spiritual experience of God delivering a spiritually dead person out of spiritual death into spiritual life. It is called the doctrine of regeneration. Regeneration is the sovereign act of God whereby He bestows upon a believing sinner new life. This is God's own life. The believing sinner becomes a partaker of God's nature. The Bible calls that a new creation. Now if a natural creation came into existence by the words of God and the national creation came into existence by the words of God how does the new creation take place in the life of a spiritually dead sinner? By the words of God. Remember Hebrews 4:12 the words of God are living, powerful, energising, penetrating. Nothing can penetrate your innermost being like the Word of God. John 5:24 the Lord Jesus said, "Verily, verily I say unto you, he that heareth my words and believeth on Him that sent me hath everlasting life and shall not come into condemnation" watch it now, "but has passed out of death into life."

In 1927 as a teenager I heard the Word of God and I passed out of spiritual death into spiritual life. Every person born into this world needs to be born again because we were not born right the first time. Romans 5:12 says, "Wherefore as by one man," Adam, "sin entered into the world, and death by sin; and so death passed upon all men, for all have sinned." You can never disassociate sin from death they are inseparably linked together. When Jesus said you must be born again it was because we were not born right the first time. We came into this world with a sin nature and we need to be born again. Now the power is in the Word of God, (Romans 10:17) "So then faith cometh by hearing," hearing in what? Someone said faith in faith, well that does not make sense. We have to have the source and object of faith. "Faith cometh by hearing and hearing by the word of God." The Word of God is living, energising, powerful, penetrating. On Christmas Day I heard the Word of God. I crumbled, I wept, I was like a weakling. I did not have a leg to stand on. The Word of God convicted me of my sin. I Peter 1:23 says, "Being born again, not of corruptible seed, but of incorruptible, by the Word of God, which liveth and abideth forever."

I have just completed 60 years in the ministry. For 60 years I have been teaching and preaching the Word of God and I have seen it work enough. I am not about to change and I am not about to retire. I have not found anything in the Bible to tell me to retire. Why? I have got a message which is alive, it works. We are on the road 48 weeks every year all over the American continent and other countries and we are seeing the Word of God work in the hearts of men and women. Thank God you have a church and a Pastor who believes and teaches this Book. Once you water it down to let in what people want, not what they need, you are in for trouble. All across our beloved nation, there is creeping into our churches this changing culture. Ministers are finding substitutes for the Word of God. If it works, use it. If they want entertainment, give them entertainment, that will get them in. It may get them in but if you win them with entertainment you are going to have to feed them with entertainment to hold them. If we win them with the Word of God we can hold them with the Word of God.

"All Scripture is given by inspiration of God and is profitable." That is the first All for our series.

AMEN AND AMEN!

The All of Sin

❖

This series of Bible messages is based on a little word of three letters; it is the most complete comprehensive word in any language, the little word A-L-L - All. We began with "All Scripture is given by inspiration of God"- 2 Timothy 3:16. I want to look at 1 Corinthians chapter 10 verse 32: "Give none offense". In this text you are going to find God's threefold division, His ethnic division of the human race. This is how God sees the human race, not by nationality, not by colour, not by race, not by denomination, this is God's threefold division of the human race: "Give none offence, neither to the Jews, nor to the Gentiles, nor to the church of God".

Everyone is either an unsaved Jew; an unsaved Gentile, or you are a member of God's church. That is God's division of the human race. By the way that has always been in your Bible. I did not put that in there.

In Matthew chapter 16, verse 18 the Lord Jesus said: "I will build my church". That is what He is doing now, building His church. In His church are saved Jews, saved Gentiles: there is no distinction in God's programme. God is not building a Kingdom, Christ is not building a Kingdom, He is building His church. We want to deal with the sin issue that keeps people out of Christ's church. This is very important, dear friends, because you or I can be a member of a local church of any denomination and not be a member of Christ's church. We will look at that subject when dealing with the All of Sin.

In Paul's epistle to the Romans he is not preaching the Gospel to unsaved people, he is teaching the Gospel to Christians. Romans was written to believers; it is the greatest masterpiece on the Gospel than any other Book in the Bible: "I am not ashamed of the Gospel of Christ; for it is the power of God unto salvation to every one that believeth; to the Jew first, and also to the Greek (or Gentile)" He is teaching the Gospel to believers. In teaching the Gospel he is dealing with Jews and Gentiles, and he makes it very clear in the Gospel record that there is no difference in the sight of God between a Jew and a Gentile. That Jew is either a member of Christ's church, that Gentile is either a member of Christ's church, or that Jew or that Gentile is lost and desperately in need of the Lord Jesus Christ and His Gospel.

In this present study the word 'All' has to do with sin. Note the frequency of the word 'All'. Speaking both to the Jews and the Gentiles, Paul said in Romans chapter 3 and verse 9: "What then? are we better than they? No, in no wise: for we have before proved both Jews and Gentiles, that they are (watch the next word) all under sin". No difference in God's plan: "they are all under sin".

During World War 1, yes, I was around in World War 1, 1914 to 1918, I was the oldest of six boys, and I was the only member in our family that caught the contagious epidemic of diphtheria; it swept all across the United States of America, and people were dying in great numbers. The Board of Health sent their representative to our little house and they put a sign on the outside, "Under quarantine". That meant that anyone in that house could not leave, and anyone outside of the house could not go in except the physician who came to visit the sick. All were under quarantine. Paul was saying here: "Whether you are a Jew or a Gentile, all are under sin".

I want you to note some of the verses here, and it is so simple. You could stumble over the simplicity of the truth in the Bible if you were not just paying attention. Look at verse 10: "As it is written, There is none righteous, no, not one". The word 'not' means 'not one'; it is the opposite from 'all': "All are under sin". How many are righteous? None, not one. If all are under sin, then not one could be righteous. You would have a contradiction of terms here. "As it is written, there is none righteous, no, not one". Verse 11: "There is none that understandeth". (By the way, these are Protestant 'nones' here) "There is none that seeketh after God". I am just reading from the Bible. "There is none, no, not one". That is quite a statement, dear friends. Do you understand what is in your Bible? Who are sinners? A-L-L. That may not sit well with you, but please accept it, it is true. Not one!

Go down to verse 23 of Romans chapter 3: "For (what is the next word?) all have sinned, and come short of the glory of God". This is a Baptist Church, and for many years I was a Baptist Pastor. For twenty-five of my sixty years in the ministry I was a Baptist Pastor. I want to ask you a simple question, I do not know whether you ever have an informal evening service, but occasionally I do not act like a preacher, I just act like a normal human being, and just get right down to where folks are. I want to ask you a very simple question, Do you believe there is a Baptist anywhere in the world who is not a sinner? You look scared! What does the Bible say? How many have sinned? How many? All! Is there a Baptist anywhere in this world who is not a sinner? No. Thank you! I have two courageous people here. Do you think there is a Presbyterian anywhere on planet earth who is not a sinner? No! Do you think there is a Methodist or an Episcopalian? Do you think there is any Protestant on the face of this earth who is not a sinner? According to the Bible the answer is 'not one': "All have sinned, and come short of the glory of God".

I am going to ask another question, do you think there is a Roman Catholic on planet earth who is not a sinner? No! Two more courageous people in the audience tonight. I want to be helpful, I came to be a blessing. Do you believe there is a Protestant minister on this earth who is not a sinner? How do you know? The Bible says "All have sinned". Do you believe there is a Roman Catholic priest on this earth who is not a sinner? I have got my Bible in my hand now dear friends. The answer is in the Book and it is in your Bible the same as it is in mine; it has always been there, I did not put it there.

Do you believe it is possible that there is a Pope on planet earth who is not a sinner? The answer is in the Bible. Do not be afraid, dear folks, it has always been there. The answer is 'No'.

This is a very important subject. God does not have more than one way, God does not have two ways, God does not have a Jewish way and a Gentile way; a Roman

Catholic way and a Protestant way: "All have sinned, and all have come short of the glory of God". No one will ever be saved until one realises he or she is lost.

There are many churchgoing people today who are self-righteous, and they go through a ritual Sunday morning after Sunday morning, but many go home and live the rest of the week like a practical atheist as though there is no God. They do not bring God into their family life, they do not bring God into their financial life, they do not bring God into their business life, they do not bring God into their social life, they live their own life, but come back the next Sunday; go through the same ritual: Roman Catholics, Greek Orthodox, Protestants go through the ritual, and live the rest of the week like a practical atheist as though there were no God.

Dear friends, what I am telling you is true, and some of you know that it is true. It is tough to face the truth of sin, and to acknowledge that we are not righteous before God, and we need to be saved.

We have the truth here in Romans chapter 3. May I give you a simple illustration. During World War 11 the automobile manufacturers were obligated to manufacture the kind of vehicles needed for war: they were manufacturing trucks and tanks and other equipment for war, and private cars for families were being manufactured in small quotas, and each automobile dealer would get a quota each month according to the kind of cars he was selling. In the town where I was pastoring there was a Roman Catholic automobile dealer, we were good friends; he handled in those days the Chrysler Corporation, (Chrysler, Plymouth, Dodge and Desoto). Now the Desoto faded out, they do not have that any more, maybe some of you are not old enough to remember that, but Chrysler did have four cars.

They now have Plymouth, Dodge and Chrysler. I did need a new car, my car was really worn out. This dear Roman Catholic, (By the way his name was Mr. Ford but he sold Chrysler products) called me one day, and he always called me Reverend, I do not like that title. Did you know that the word 'Reverend' appears only one time in the Bible? and the only time it is used, it is one of God's Names, only God is Reverend. He did not know any better, and I did not criticize him, but he called me one day, and said, "Reverend, I have my quota of automobiles, I have two Plymouth cars, I am selling one to my priest, and I would like to sell the other to a certain minister in this town that I like". That was an honour to have that man recognise me in that way. He said, "There won't be any under-the-table money, it is going to be just on the level, I need your car, there is a demand for good used cars". I said, "I will be over to look at the car".

He said, "You will have to hurry, because I have an appointment with my priest" So I went over and looked at the car, and we were talking and he said, "Oh, I'm late for my appointment", he said, "The father is expecting me". I said, "Oh, is your father living?". He said, "Oh, the priest in our church, we have an appointment" I said, "What is the appointment for?" He said, "I go to confession, and I am due to be there to confess my sins". I thought for a moment, I said to him, "Mr. Ford, to whom does your priest confess his sins?". He said, "I'm not sure but I would guess, to the bishop". I said, "And to whom does the bishop confess his sins?". He said, "Oh, I think it is to the cardinal". "To whom does the cardinal confess his sins?". He said, "I suppose to the pope". I said, "Sir, to whom does the pope confess his sins?". He said, "I suppose to God". I said, "My dear man, there is a Man in Heaven right now, seated at the right hand of God the Father, the only Man on planet earth who never sinned. His name is Jesus Christ, He is not merely a Priest; He is not merely a Great Priest. He is the Great High Priest, and He died for your sins and for my sins, and without Him you will never make it to Heaven, no matter how many sins you confess to another sinner". The Sinless Man who died on the cross to take your guilt, your penalty, my guilt, my penalty, rose again from the dead and His Resurrection is a guarantee that all who come to God through Him will be saved. "I am the Resurrection and the Life, he that believeth in Me, though he were dead, spiritually or physically, shall have everlasting life."

Yes, dear friends, we are all under sin; every one of us. Now we are not sinners because we sin, we sin because we are sinners. You see, we were born with the sin nature. When God created Adam and Eve they were in His likeness and image, and God said to them, "Be fruitful and multiply." In other words, one of the purposes for the marriage relationship was to multiply, to have children. God said, "Be fruitful and multiply and fill up the earth" That 'fill up the earth' has to be thought of very carefully. I remember my older son, he is in Heaven now, he died three years ago at the age of sixty, and I remember when his first child was born. He was in Texas, I was in Pennsylvania, and he called me long distance on the phone about 1 o' clock in the morning, it was a collect call. He said, "Congratulations Dad" I said, "On what?" He said, "Mary just gave birth to a child". I said, "Thank you". I paid for the call, of course, and then less than two years later I had another call, and he said, "Congratulations Dad". It was collect again. I began to wonder how often is this going to happen? The fourth time I made a little remark to which he replied, "Dad, you know what the Bible says, 'Be fruitful and multiply.'" I said, "Yes, but God didn't intend one man to do it all".

God said to Adam and to Eve, "Be fruitful and multiply". That is one of the purposes for the marriage relationship. Now, if Adam and Eve could have had a child before they sinned, that child would have been a sinless, perfect child. Why? Nine times on the first page in your Bible you will read the statement, "After its kind" Everything reproduces after its kind. Diane and I went through Genesis chapter 1 yesterday again, and she sat with a pen and underlined every time we came to that phrase "after his kind". Dear friends, if Adam and Eve could have had a child before they sinned, he would have been a perfect, sinless child after its parents. But the baby was born after they sinned; they are now spiritually dead. God said to Adam, "Adam, of every tree in the garden thou mayest freely eat, but of the tree which is in the midst of the garden thou shalt not eat of it, for in the day that thou eatest thereof thou shalt surely die". The moment Adam ate the fruit he died spiritually; he alienated himself from God. God said, "You will die", and he died spiritually; cut himself off from the life of God. He was spiritually dead. Physically alive but spiritually dead. My dear friends, every baby born into this world is born with a nature just like Adam, just like Eve.

We never had any girls in our house. My son had four boys. I had two sons. The only girls we have are the girls that the boys married, but my older son who is in Heaven now had a rough time: he was a premature baby and really gave us a tough time. That little guy cried constantly, and I wanted to be a help so I would pick up the baby at night and carry him, and pat him, and walk him, and when I thought he would be asleep I tiptoed over to his crib, tucked him in, pulled up the blanket, get back to bed, pull up my cover and, my, he would start all over again. One day my mother said, "Son, do not be alarmed at Richard". I said, "Why not?" She said, "You cried the first year of your life, he is a chip of the old block". We never had a girl, but if we had and she had cried once I would have said, "There's a feather out of the old hen". All of our children came into the world with a nature just like mother and daddy, that is the way you came, that is the way your children and your grandchildren came, with a sin nature, and the only baby born into this world who was not born with a sin nature is the Holy Son of God; He did not have a human father, He was supernaturally conceived in the womb of a virgin; He escaped the sin nature, the sin principle. Jesus Christ never sinned. In my study of our Lord Jesus Christ I will add to that, whether you all want to agree with me or not, not only is it true that Jesus did not sin, but Jesus Christ could not sin. He escaped the sin nature, He did not have a human father.

You see, the male sperm is essential for every conception, and Mary never knew a man. Christ was supernaturally conceived by the power of the Holy Spirit, He never sinned and never could sin. Now if Jesus Christ could sin here on earth He could sin now in Heaven. Hebrews chapter 13, verse 8: "Jesus Christ the same yesterday, and today, and for ever". He is immutable. God cannot change, Christ is God, He cannot change, He could not sin. God cannot be tempted with evil, neither tempteth He any man. God does not tempt us, and we cannot tempt God. I do not test God either. I never put God to the test. I do not test God, I trust God. I do not have to put Him to the test, I know He is faithful, I know He is righteous, I know He is true, I know He is merciful, I know He pities us.

I can trust God, I never test God, never, I would not dare test God but I can always trust God.

The Lord Jesus Christ is the only sinless person who ever visited planet earth, and He is the Man seated at God's right hand. Now Romans chapter 5 and verse 12 says: "Wherefore, as by one man (Adam) sin entered into the world, and death by sin".

You can never disassociate sin from death. Romans chapter 6, verse 23: "For the wages of sin is death". Ezekiel chapter 18, verse 4: "The soul that sinneth, it shall die". James chapter 1, verse 15: "Sin, when it is finished, bringeth forth death". You can never disassociate sin from death.

Every unsaved person is spiritually dead, alienated, cut off from the life of God. It has always been in your Bible, I did not put that there, dear friends, it has always been there.

Why do you think the Lord Jesus said, "Ye must be born again"? Because we were not born right the first time. My mother had a sin nature. My daddy had a sin nature. When I was born I received a sin nature. David said, "I was shapen in iniquity, and in sin did my mother conceive me". (Psalm 51). He is not saying that the marital relation between his mother and father was sinful, he is simply saying, "My father had a sin nature, my mother had a sin nature." When I was conceived and born of my parents, everything reproduces after its kind. I was born with a sin nature. We do not have to send our children to a crime school to teach them how to lie or steal. Let us be honest now. Do not tell me you had a child that never lied to you.

If you told me that I would question whether you can tell the truth. All of us parents know that at one time or another our children tell lies. Where did they learn that?

Did we send them to a crime school to teach them how to sin? No, they are born with a built-in sin system, just like yours, just like mine, and that sin alienates us from God. That is why the Lord Jesus Christ came from Heaven. Matthew chapter 1, verse 21 says, "Thou shalt call His Name Jesus: for He shall save His people from their sins". There is no answer to the sin question, dear friends, apart from the Lord Jesus Christ the sinless Son of God.

I love the epistle to the Hebrews; In chapter 1 you have seven proofs for the Deity of Christ. In chapter 2 you have seven proofs for the Humanity of Christ. So the epistle opens by introducing the *Perfect Son*. You read on through seven or eight chapters and you come to the *Perfect Son who offered the Perfect Sacrifice*, and you read on and discover that the *Perfect Son* who offered the Perfect Sacrifice provides a *Perfect Salvation*. "Neither is there salvation in any other: for there is none other name under Heaven given among men, whereby we must be saved". (Acts 4:12). God has one way of saving people. Please, dear friends, it is not a Protestant way or a Roman Catholic way, a Jewish way or a Gentile way, no, Jesus said, "I am the Way, the Truth and the Life, no man cometh unto the Father but by Me". We have to come to see the truth of God's Word. It is so simple, we could stumble over its simplicity. Now one thing will keep an unsaved person from admitting he or she is a sinner and is willing to be saved, and that is the word pride: that is a tough one to handle. Who wants to admit they are sinners? None of us! Pride will grip us every time we are under conviction, and we sense the need of deliverance from our sins. The noun 'salvation', the verb 'saved' and the title 'Saviour' appears in your Bible more than one hundred times. It could be used in reference to saving someone from dying. Peter was walking on the water, and the Lord bid Peter to come and Peter began to walk on the water, he took his eyes off Jesus and began to sink. Realising he was drowning he cried out the shortest prayer in the Bible: "Lord, save me", and Jesus saved him. That was salvation from physical death.

When a sinner realises he or she is lost and needs to be saved, pride will not keep them, I hope, from saying "Lord, save me". "Him that cometh unto me I will in no wise cast out".

I must repeat it again for emphasis, God has only one way of saving people, and any who are not saved, this is God's way, fight it if you will, you will be a loser every time. Jesus said, "I am the Way, the Truth and the Life, no man cometh unto the Father but by me".

That is the All of sin, no one has escaped it. No religious leader in all the world has escaped sin. Why? "All have sinned and come short of the glory of God." Perhaps one of the greatest salvation passages in the Old Testament is Isaiah chapter 53, the verse begins like this, "All we like sheep have gone astray, we have turned every one to his own way". "All have sinned", every one, that is the meaning of the word 'all'. None are excluded. "All have sinned and come short of the glory of God". There are none righteous, no, not one.

I trust, dear friends, that if you are saved you might catch a vision of concern for your dear loved ones. One of the burdens on my heart and the heart of my wife are some unsaved loved ones very near, very precious to us, and we know that if they die in rejection of Christ they have made the choice to go to hell. God will never send any one to hell, and may I say at this point that God never pre-destinated any one to go to hell. The word 'predestination' is never used in the Bible of an unsaved person, not once.

I was preaching in Grand Rapids, Michigan, and the pastor preached a sermon the week before I arrived to prepare the people, and announced my coming, some people came to the church who were not members, and one man said to me, after I had preached at the Sunday evening service, "Would you be my guest for lunch tomorrow?" I said, "Yes, I can arrange that". He said, "I will pick you up at your Motel". He picked me up and we went to a restaurant and we sat down, got a menu and placed our order, and the food was delivered to us. He was in church the night before, and I assumed that he might be a Christian, but I did not know, and being his guest I waited for him to make the first move, not to pick up the cheque, but whether we were going to thank God for the food or not. I just waited a few moments, and he picked up his utensils and began to arrange to eat. I just very unassumedly just bowed my head and offered a quiet word of thanks for my food, I always thank God for my food. If you are a professing Christian tonight, please thank God for your food, and will you take this kindly, if you do not thank God for your food you do not deserve it. There are millions of people on planet earth who are dying with starvation tonight. Thank God for your food. I thought I would start a conversation with the dear man, and I said to him: "Tell me about your salvation. When and how did you become a Christian?" That is always a good starter if you want to get into conversation. "Oh" he said, "I never bother about that". He said, "If God predestinated me to get to heaven I will get there, and if God pre-destinated me to go to hell I will have to go there". My heart went out to that poor ignorant church man. Ladies and gentlemen, nowhere in your Bible is it ever intimated that God ever predestinated anybody to go to hell. The word is never used of an unsaved person. Look at it carefully in Paul's Letter to the Ephesians chapter 1 and Romans chapter 8. If any one ends up in hell, believe me, dear friend, it is because you chose to go to hell. God has made a way of escape. He does not want any one lost, He wants all to be saved, but He has only one Way of saving people. "Neither is there salvation in any other: for there is none other name under Heaven given among men, whereby we must be saved", and that Name is the Lord Jesus Christ.

In our next message we have good news. This was the bad news in our message; All are sinners, but our next message; How can I be saved? If I get saved will I know that I am saved? If I get salvation could I ever lose it? That will be our study.

This message, "The All of Sin". Our next message, "The All of Christ". Pray for your loved ones, dear friends, if they are not saved they are making a choice to go to hell. Maybe God will use our readings to help dear people who are not saved to receive Christ and be guaranteed of eternal life.

AMEN AND AMEN!

The All of Christ

❖

This series has been revolving around the most inclusive word in any language, it is the little word 'All' - A-L-L. We began our series with 2 Timothy 3:16: "All Scripture is given by inspiration of God". Our first study on the word 'All' was the Scriptures. The second 'All' we dealt with was the doctrine of sin: "All have sinned, and have come short of the glory of God".

Now, we are going to deal with the Saviour.

Turn in your Bible to Colossians chapter 3. I am going to look at a couple of verses beginning with verse 9: "Lie not one to another, seeing that ye have put off the old man with his deeds; And have put on the new man, which is renewed in knowledge after the image of Him that created him. Where there is neither Greek nor Jew, circumcision nor uncircumcision, Barbarian, Scythian, bond nor free: but Christ is all, and in all".

Turn back to chapter 1, the text came from Colossians chapter 3, the exposition will be in chapter 1. I do not know if the apostle Paul ever visited the city of Colosse in Asia Minor, and you do not know if he did, because in his missionary journeys we are never told whether Paul was there or not, but he had a dear friend living there who kept him informed of things going on in the assembly there. Then, of course, he had the Holy Spirit directing him to write.

I want you to look at Colossians chapter 1, and we want to see the 'All' of our Saviour. We begin this interest-ing, and informative and instructive chapter with Paul's prelude. He introduces this Book with the following words: "Paul, an apostle of Jesus Christ by the will of God". He was not a self-appointed apostle, he was an apostle called by the will of God and in the will of God.

"Paul, an apostle of Jesus Christ by the will of God". Dear friend, the best place for us is in the will of God. Dear Christian brothers and sisters, the greatest tragedy that could come to anyone of us in this meeting is to live and die and cross the stage of human experience and fail to find and follow and finish up in the will of God. I do not want to die out of the will of God. Thank you Paul, it is nice to hear from a man who is in the will of God.

Then he is very generous: he speaks of Timotheus, or Timothy his brother, who was much younger than Paul. Paul had a love for younger pastors. Now he is writing to the saints and faithful brethren in Christ. We must rescue this word 'saint' from its misuse today. Unfortunately, many people who go to church do not understand the meaning of the word 'saint'. The word 'saint' is one of the many names and titles given to Christians. We are sons of God, we are said to be saved, we are stewards, we are sheep.

There are many names and titles beginning with the letter 's' but the word 'saint' is most important, it is the noun form of the verb 'sanctified', and it simply means to set apart. A saint is a set-apart person. Every Christian is a saint. Somebody wants to know who is speaking at Iron Hall. Tell them saint Lehman Strauss was here, I can prove that from the Bible. If you say you are a saint that is a title that God has given to every believer. You do not become a saint after you die. Nobody can canonise you after you are dead. Saints are not made on the other side of the grave, they are made in this life. Only God can make a saint out of a sinner. No church can make a saint out of a sinner, only God makes saints. Paul is writing to believers, to the saints. *Now beginning with verse 3 we have Paul's praise of the saints.* There was something about the believers in Colosse that impressed Paul, and the Spirit of God used that to guide him in the writing of this letter.

Let us see now what Paul found, he is not bragging on the saints. He is not praising the saints, he is praising God for the saints. He is not patting them on the back, he is praising God for them. Verse 3: "We give thanks to God and the Father of our Lord Jesus Christ, praying always for you, since we heard of your (oh, mark this, mark the word 'faith', and mark the word 'love' in verse 4, and mark the word 'hope' in verse 5). *There were three things that characterised the saints in Colosse. One was a faith that was not secret.* Paul said, "We are hearing of your faith". Has anyone heard of yours lately? Has anyone heard of my faith in Christ lately? It is commendable, beloved, and when those who are hearing of our faith also see us back it up with a life, it is going to make a mark in this world and sinners will become saints through a testimony like this. A faith that was not secret! People were hearing of it. "We heard of your faith".

Then, secondly, they had a love that was not partial. Notice, it was a love to all the saints. Oh, I would like to have been a pastor of a church like that where everybody loved everybody; no cliques, no little separations, no divisions, that is the way it was. Everybody loved everybody in the church in Colosse; they had a love that was not partial. A faith that was not secret, and a love that was not partial. *Watch verse 5, they had a hope which was not misplaced.* Now, Heaven was not their hope, their hope was in Heaven, and in this epistle Paul tells us that hope is not a place, hope is a Person. "Christ in you, the hope of Glory". What do you have your hope in my friend? In what or in whom are you pinning your hope? Hope never deals with the past, you do not hope for anything in the past. Hope is always associated with the future. "My hope is built on nothing less, than Jesus' Blood and Righteousness!" They had a hope that was not misplaced. Their hope was in Heaven, and that hope, the Person, is coming back to receive His own unto Himself. Paul's praise of the saints! Now they were not perfect. No Christian is perfect. There was a perfect man and a perfect woman united in marriage, and they were placed in a perfect environment, and you would think that a perfect man and a perfect woman in a perfect environment would lead to a perfect society. That perfect couple, that was Adam and Eve, but they blew it, they disobeyed God. You can put a good man and a good woman in a good environment but, my friend, without Christ there is no hope.

Let us see what Paul is going to do next. *After praising God for the saints he is going to pray to God for the saints.* Look at verse 9: "For this cause we also, since the day we heard it, do not cease to pray for you". *What is he going to pray for?* "and to desire that ye might be filled with the knowledge of God's will".* Mark the word 'will' in your Bible, we mentioned it here in verse 1, "the will of God". The will of God is described with three adjectives in Romans chapter 12: "I beseech you therefore, brethren, by the mercies of God, that ye present your bodies a living sacrifice, holy, acceptable unto God, which is your reasonable service. And be not conformed to this world: but be ye transformed by the renewing of your mind,(Watch it!) that ye may prove what is that good, and acceptable, and perfect will of God". Think of those three adjectives: can you improve on that? "Good, acceptable, and perfect". That is the Bible's description of the will of God. I do not want to miss that. You can't improve on that. Paul says, "I am praying for you. I am praying for you that ye might be filled with the knowledge of His will".

Mark the next word beginning with the letter 'w' and the word is 'wisdom'. 'God's will in all wisdom and spiritual understanding'. James chapter 1 verse 5: "If any of you lack wisdom. let him ask of God". There are many different kinds of wisdom in this world, but, my dear friends, it is best to have the wisdom of God than the wisdom of man. We cannot trust in man, but we can trust in God, we can believe God.

Let us look then at verse 10. *What else was he praying for? "That ye might walk worthy of the Lord". He was praying for God's will, for God's wisdom, and for their walk.* Now the word 'walk' is not used literally. In order for me to get to this platform I walked through a door out there; walked over here; walked up a few steps and a few more steps, and then I walked one more step up to where I am now. That is how I got here: by walking. That is not the meaning of the word 'walk'. It is not the way we carry ourselves physically from one geographical location to another, it is how we carry ourselves morally, ethically, spiritually. It is the behaviour of the Christian.

Paul says "I am praying for your walk, that ye might walk worthy of the Lord unto all pleasing". That is not pleasing all people. Nobody can please all people and please God. Walk worthy of the Lord pleasing God in all things.

Are we pleasing the Lord, or are we men pleasers? Paul said, "If I seek to please men I can't be the servant of Christ". No pastor can please everybody in the church and be Christ's true servant, it is impossible, we can't do it dear friends. I have been a pastor for many years, I quit trying, I would end up in a mental institution if I spent all of my life trying to please people. People's demands are different; their desires are different, you can't please people. Oh, beloved, we can please God, and when we are pleasing Him we are on top with Him. Paul said, "I am praying for you, praying that ye might find God's will, I am praying that ye might be filled with God's wisdom, and I am praying that ye might walk worthy of the Lord unto all pleasing". Mark the word 'will', and mark the word 'wisdom', and mark the word 'walk', *and then in verse 10 mark the word 'work'*. See it? By the way that has always been in your Bible, I did not put those words there. "That ye might walk worthy of the Lord unto all pleasing, being fruitful in every good work, and increasing in the knowledge of God". It is nice to have saints in God's will walking with God, getting involved in God's work; that makes for a healthy Christian. Spiritual growth is marked by the will of God, the wisdom of God, a walk with God and a work for God. How are we doing in our church? How does it stack up with the church in Colosse?

Well, we have the prelude to the epistle. A few comments on Paul's praise of the saints. Then a few comments on Paul's prayer for the saints. I want to bring you to the lesson of the evening; *Paul's portrait of the Saviour.* One of the loveliest portraits of the Lord Jesus is found in Colossians chapter 1. There is one in Ephesians chapter 1. There is an excellent portrait in Revelation chapter 1, but here in Colossians chapter 1 is a pen-portrait of the Lord Jesus Christ, and every description of Christ in the rest of this passage contains two words, "All things". This is the Christ of Colossians.

Let us look at some of these verses and see the Saviour.

"Christ is all", chapter 3, verse 11. I am reading from verse 12 of chapter 1: "Giving thanks unto the Father, which hath made us meet(or fit) to be partakers of the inheritance of the saints in light: Who hath delivered us from the power of darkness, and hath translated us into the kingdom of His dear Son. In whom we have redemption through His Blood, even the forgiveness of sins". Keep your pen handy and mark the "All things"; every one refers to some aspect of the Life and Work of the Lord Jesus Christ. I am reading now from verse 15: "Who is the image of the *Invisible* God, the firstborn of every creature: For by Him were all things created". *The first "all things" of the Saviour in Colossians chapter 1. After that statement write "His power"*: He created all things. John chapter 1, verse 1: "In the beginning was the Word, and the Word was with God, and the Word was God. The same was in the beginning with God. All things were made by Him; and without Him was not anything made that was made". He was there in the beginning with the Father and the Holy Spirit, and He was active in the creation of this world. Your Saviour put it all together. His power!

Let us read on, and look at the "All things" as we go along. "For by Him were all things created, that are in heaven, and that are in earth, visible and invisible. whether they be thrones, or dominions, or principalities, or powers" (Colossians 1:16) Watch it now, another "all things", Christ is all: "All things were created by Him, and for Him"

(Colossians 1:16). Not *only do you see* His *power, but what* He *created they are* His *possessions*; they were created by Him and for Him. He says, "The cattle upon a thousand hills are mine, the gold and the silver is mine".

Do you think you own anything beloved Christian? I do not! There may be a few things and I may hold a title to them, maybe there is no debt on them, and maybe you have some property on planet earth, and you hold a Title Deed to it, it is debt-free. Maybe you have an automobile or two and they are paid for, and you have a title to those automobiles. I do not know what you have, you do not know what I have, but I will tell you one thing, dear friend, we do not own anything: we are stewards, we are custodians, we are caretakers.

Listen carefully. God may not take from us what we have but just as sure as you are in this meeting tonight one day God will take us from it, and do not ever forget it my friend. Whose is it then? We are stewards, we are caretakers, we are custodians. My time is in God's hand. Anything He has loaned to me, or put in trust with me is His, and all that will be in heaven waiting for me when I get there is what I sent on ahead, nothing more, nothing less, nothing different. We are stewards, and it is required of stewards that a man or a woman be found faithful. Are we trustworthy with all that God has entrusted to us? They are His possessions. It is a wonderful thing to know God when I deal with God's supply. We dealt with a couple of key words dealing with the letter 'S' in the "Alls". We have the "All" of Scripture, and the "All" of sin, and the "All" of the Saviour, but one night, the Lord willing, we will deal with the "All" of God's supply: "My God shall supply all your need". Does that not awaken me to the fact that if God has guaranteed to supply all my need, am I going to worry about it? The

Bible says, God "never slumbers nor sleeps". Now there is no point in both of us staying awake at night worrying about what my needs are going to be tomorrow, and how they are going to be met. My Heavenly Father has promised to take care of all our tomorrows. Why do we not trust Him? "All things are created by Him, and for Him", they are His possessions.

Let us look on down, "Verse 16: "For by Him were all things created, that are in heaven, and that are in earth, visible and invisible, whether they be thrones or dominions, or principalities, or powers: all things were created by Him, and for Him". Let us look on to verse 17 "And He is before all things", that is His pre-existence. There is a teaching abroad, it is incorrect, and it is beginning to spread around and filter out, it goes under a name, somebody gave it, 'Incarnational Sonship': that 'Jesus Christ is not the Eternal Son of God. He became the Son of God at His Incarnation'. Ladies and gentleman, that is touching dangerously on the Deity of Christ. He is the Eternal Son of God, it is right there in your Bible my friend: "He is before all things". The Birth of Jesus Christ is not the beginning of the Son of God. He is before all things, His pre-existence. (I will say it again) To say that Jesus Christ became the Son of God at His Incarnation is touching dangerously on the Deity of Christ. Stick with your Bible dear friends: "In the beginning was the Word" In the beginning, yes! "And the Word was with God, and the Word was God". Who is the Word? The second Person of the Godhead - "The Eternal Son". He is before all things, His pre-existence.

Now verse 17 again. "He is before all things, and by Him (Here is another "all things") all things consist". *They hold together, His Providence*: what He creates He controls. He created this universe and He holds it together. It is wonderful! I do not know much about science, it was never one of my majors, I did not have many majors, most of them were minors, but I managed to get through with a couple of them, but I know this much, and I have said it in Universities to young people : If little planet earth could drift off its course and drift slightly toward the sun, every human body would melt with the atomic energy of the sun. We could not survive it. Or if our little earth were to drift too far away from the sun, in a matter of a short time we would freeze to death, we could not survive, but it will never happen. The God who put it together is the God who holds it together. "By Him all things consist". His Providence! This is your Saviour. This is the Man Christ who is All.

Let us look again at the text: "By Him all things consist" They hold together, "And He is the head of the body, the church"(Verse 18). This is the One who is All, this is the One who created and who controls, and who will claim all things. When He comes back He will claim what is His. Then every knee will bow, and every tongue confess that Jesus Christ is Lord to the Glory of God the Father. It is all in the Book dear friends. What a Saviour!

Let us go on, there is a little more here that we have to see before we conclude our study. Verse 17 says "By Him all things consist", and He is the head of the body, the church. You know who is the Head of the church? I will use this illustration: When I began my ministry as a pastor I was young and I did not know much, and I am conducting the first annual business meeting of the Calvary Baptist Church in Bristol, Pennsylvania. It is a newly organised church, I am the first pastor. I never was taught in the Bible College how to conduct a business meeting in the church, I never had a course in that. Here I am now a young pastor,

not yet thirty years of age, and I am before my congrega-
tion and we are now going to have our first annual business meeting. I am standing up here and I am just saying
to myself, "Lord, please help me to say something tonight
that makes sense". Something came to my mind and I can't
tell you how. It is not original with me because I never had
an original thought in my life, never. I am serious, everything I know I learned somewhere from someone, but somewhere I got the idea of placing a chair down here in the
front before the audience, and I said, "Dear folks, this chair,
this vacant chair represents the unseen head of this church,
I am not the head of the church." I said, "None of you
sitting down there is the head of this church." Now what I
said next I am ashamed of, I am just being honest with you
and it is not to provoke any amusement. What I said I
wished I would have said differently. I said, "Before anyone
stands up and spouts off." (I would not say that today. I
would say, "Before you rise to speak." I have grown a few
years and I have matured a little bit). I am not proud of
saying, "Before you stand up and spout off, take a look at
that chair. The head of this church is the Lord Jesus Christ.
We are members of His Body, and if every member is in
subjection to the Head this church will never have a split".
They invited me back for the fiftieth anniversary, and they
were still together and growing. They never forgot the first
annual business meeting. Now this story may sound like a
boast. I hope you won't take it as a boast. I am normally
proud like the rest of you, we are born with a proud system
built in us. But they brought me back for the fiftieth
anniversary and made me Pastor Emeritus. I had been away
for all those years, I did not even know what the word
'Emeritus' meant. I said to the Pastor, 'What is this
Emeritus thing here? Is it anything like arthritis?' He said,

'That is Pastor Emeritus'. I said, 'Well, what does it mean?'. He said, 'You can't vote, you do not get any pay, we just put your name on the letter head and use you'. That is what they do. My name is still on the letter head. Every time I go back to that church, and recently I took Diane back there, it is thrilling to see that church after fifty-five years and not one split. They were taught that Christ is the head of the church. A body has only one head.

When Ronald Regan was President of the USA he appointed a friend of mine, Dr. C. Everett Koop as the Surgeon General. His responsibilities covered all the medical aspects of our nation including the Drug Department.

Dr. Koop was the first man to separate Siamese twins successfully. He was a devout Christian and I knew him well back in the time when he was the Director of Saint Luke's Childrens Hospital in the city of Philadelphia. He told me that he was so thankful that God allowed him to separate the Siamese twins.

You know a body with two heads would be a freak of nature. Years ago circuses and shows would have paid big money to make sport of a body with two heads. Now the lesson is, my friends a body with two heads is a monstrosity. God gave His Son to be the head of the church which is His body. Christ is the sole King and head of His Church.

If every member was in subjection to the head you would never have a split; you will never have any shame on your church, and people do not forget Christians who can't get along with each other, they do not forget the church that can't live with itself.

Colossians chapter 1, verse 18. Let us take two more 'all things' here. While we are on the subject of the head, let me finish verse 18: "Who is the beginning, the firstborn from the dead; that in all things He might have the preeminence". *Go back over the 'all things': you have His Power, His Possessions, His Providence, His Preeminence.* You know what the word 'preeminence' means? Number one, The word 'preeminence' appears only one other time in the New Testament; In the little third epistle of John there was a man by the name of Diotrephes who loved to have the preeminence. You know what he said? 'I am number one in this church. John is coming through but I will do the preaching, let the apostle John take a side seat. I am preeminent in this church'. That is the only other use of the word 'preeminence' in the New Testament. It makes me sad to tell you, a leader in a local assembly had to be number one, had to have the preeminence.

Beloved, that in all things He, Christ, might have the preeminence. Christ is all. I am going to close with one more: Verse 20, "And, having made peace through the Blood of His Cross". If you are saved you have peace with God. Romans 5:1: "Therefore being justified by faith, we have peace with God". Every saved person has peace with God.

When I was a patient in the hospital. In the States we call it 'The Expensive Care Unit'. Some places it is called 'The Intensive Care Unit'. When I was in the Expensive Care Unit, and had a couple of private nurses, and one of them was a Christian, and when she would come into my room knowing my condition she would sometimes pray, and one day she said to me, "Pastor Strauss, there is a man, a patient here in the hospital and he is having a strange kind of a stroke whereby he can hear me but he can't respond" She said, "Today, I just leaned over close to his ear, and I asked him this, 'Have you made your peace with God?'" I do not know what she expected from me but I said, "Tell me, suppose he could have answered you and said, 'No, I have not made my peace with God. Can you please tell me how I can do this?' what would you have told him? She did not know, because you can't make your peace with God, you can't make peace with God, Christ "made peace through the blood of His cross". There needed to be a reconciliation. We must be reconciled to God. God does not need to be reconciled to us, we are the wayward ones, we need to be reconciled to God. When you come to Christ and receive Him you have peace with God.

There is one other thing I want to say in conclusion. Do all of us Christians enjoy the peace of God? Oh, you have peace with God, that is your position. Having been justified by faith, declared righteous by God you have peace with God, but are we enjoying and experiencing the peace of God? I trust Philippians 4: 6 and 7: "Be anxious for nothing, Do not worry about anything, but in everything and supplication with thanksgiving let your requests be made known unto God. And the peace of God which passeth all understanding will guard your heart and your mind through Christ Jesus" Christ is all! Let us draw nigh to Him, beloved, from day to day, walking in unbroken fellowship with Him, and, friend, if you have never received the Lord Jesus Christ as your Saviour you are missing all, for everything you ever need in time and for eternity is bound up in the Person and Work of the Lord Jesus Christ. Christ is all!

AMEN AND AMEN!

The All of Salvation

---❖---

We have been using in our messages the little three-lettered word, the most inclusive word in any language, the little word 'All'. We considered the 'All' of the Scriptures: "All scripture is given by inspiration of God".

We considered the 'All' of sin: "All have sinned and come short of the glory of God". We considered the 'All' of our Saviour: Colossians 3:9, "Christ is all and in all". We are going to consider the 'All' of Salvation.

Our text is 2 Peter 3:9: "The Lord is not ... willing that any perish, but that all should come to repentance".

Now, the subject is Salvation. Your Bible is opened to Exodus chapter 14: I would like to look at a couple of verses from this chapter, one in the middle of the chapter and the other at the end of the chapter, I am reading from verse 13:

"Moses said unto the people, Fear ye not, stand still, and see the salvation of the Lord, which He will shew to you today: for the Egyptians whom ye have seen today, ye shall see them again no more for ever. The Lord shall fight for you, and ye shall hold your peace". Look at verse 30: "Thus the Lord saved Israel that day out of the hand of the Egyptians; and Israel saw the Egyptians dead upon the sea shore". Now in verse 13 of chapter 14 you have the noun 'salvation'. In verse 30 of the same chapter you have the verb 'saved'. Let us begin by discussing briefly the meaning of salvation. When we speak about salvation what are we talking about? Well, actually, the noun 'salvation' and the verb 'saved' comes to us from a Latin word: it is the word 'salvos' from which we get our English word 'Salvage'. To salvage something is to save something. When I was a boy in the Pennsylvania Dutch country we had men in business who had, what we called in those days, junk yards: they would buy anything, any old junk, and if it was just a wrecked car with a wheel on it that could be salvaged they would buy that wrecked car to salvage the wheel. Or it could be an old icebox before the electric refrigerators came in, and when the electric refrigerators came in the old iceboxes were sold to the junk men, but they were always saving them lest somebody needed a door to an icebox. They call them salvage companies now, they do not call them junk yards anymore. What did they do? They salvaged something, they saved something. Now the word 'save' and 'salvation' comes from the Latin 'salvage'- to salvage means to save something.

In the passage before us it meant to save Israel from death at the hands of the Egyptians. Moses said, "Stand still, and see the salvation of the Lord". See how God will rescue you; God will save you; God will deliver you. Then across the page we read "And the Lord saved Israel"- He rescued Israel, He salvaged Israel, He saved Israel. The meaning of the word 'salvation'.

Turn to the same chapter in a New Testament Book, the Gospel according to Matthew, and again find chapter 14. There is an interesting and informative story of human interest, and you all know what it is all about when we get to it. I want to read from Matthew chapter 14, beginning with verse 22, "And straightway Jesus constrained His disciples to get into a ship, and to go before Him unto the other side, while He sent the multitude away. And when He had sent the multitudes away, He went up into a mountain apart to pray: and when the evening was come, He was there alone. But the ship was now in the midst of the sea, tossed with waves: for the wind was contrary. And in the fourth watch of the night Jesus went unto them walking on the sea. When the disciples saw Him walking on the sea, they were troubled, saying, It is a spirit". They thought they were looking at a ghost. "And they cried out for fear. But straightway Jesus spake unto them, saying, Be of good cheer; it is I; be not afraid. And Peter answered Him and said, Lord, if it be Thou, (if this is really you) bid me to come unto Thee on the water. And He said, Come. And when Peter was come down out of the ship, he walked on the water, to go to Jesus. But when he saw the wind boisterous, he was afraid;" (That means he took his eyes off the Lord). "and beginning to sink" You have one of the shortest prayers in the Bible, and Jesus answered that prayer. What is the prayer? "Lord, save me". Have you ever asked God to save you? No one on planet earth ever asked God to save them and was turned away from the Lord. That is the shortest prayer in the Bible: "Lord, save me".

Salvation in the scriptures does not refer to being salvaged or rescued from physical danger or death, it has to do with eternal salvation. It is used in a spiritual sense, and the reason why scripture has so much to say about salvation is because it is the means of rescuing people from the penalty of sin.

In our study on the subject of sin we learned that there is not a human being on planet earth who is not a sinner. All have sinned and have come short of the glory of God. The tragedy is that people, many of them who are not saved do not know that they are lost, and if you are not saved then you are lost. Luke 19, verse 10: "The Son of Man is come to seek and to save that which was lost". Every unsaved person is lost, and the person who is lost will never be saved until he or she realises that they are lost, and will ask God in a simple prayer: "Lord, save me".

Let me bring to you some thoughts on the means of salvation. If I am lost and need to be saved, if I am spiritually lost and on my way to eternal separation from God, what are the means of salvation? Before God could save anyone the sin question had to be dealt with. God never sweeps sin under the rug dear friends, we try to do it and get away with it, but not God. It is interesting to read through the Bible and find out how God even mentions the names of men and women who have wilfully, deliberately, intentionally sinned and rejected Him. God puts their names in the Bible, many of them. Beloved friends, God has the names of every person on planet earth. Every one born into this world is registered in God's Book, every person has his or her name in God's Register of the living. That name is there until it is blotted out. Some names will be blotted out of that Book, others will not. The only names who will be blotted out of the Book of Life -the Register of the living are the names of those who refused not to be saved; who wanted to continue lost. The sin question had to be dealt with. God is merciful and God is a God of love, God is gracious, and God does not choose to have one unsaved person go into eternity lost and separated from Him forever, that is not the will of God. God is not willing that any should perish, but that all should come to repentance. Are you among the 'All'. God is not willing that any should perish, but that all should come to repentance. Have you come? Are you saved? If not, let us discuss briefly the means of salvation.

Before any one could be saved, the sin question had to be dealt with, and so God devised the plan to deal with your sins and my sins. Now that debt of sin you and I could never pay, but God in His grace, His love and His mercy planned and provided for a means of our salvation, and so He sent His Son. The Father sent His Son the Lord Jesus Christ to be the Saviour of the world. There is not one person on planet earth for whom Christ did not die. He took upon Himself the full penalty of your sins and mine. That does not automatically save us, it means we must recognise two things. Number one: I am a sinner, and number two: My only hope for heaven is the Saviour who died for my sins. It is just as simple as that.

Now we have something of the meaning of salvation: To rescue, to salvage, to deliver from death; spiritually to deliver from eternal separation from God. Now we are going to look a little bit at the means of salvation. We read in Matthew chapter 1 verse 21: "Thou shalt call His Name Jesus: for He shall save His people from their sins". Jesus: Saviour: He shall save His people from what? From the penalty and the guilt of sin, Matthew 1:21.

Do you know what Mary said when Jesus was Born? She said, "This is God my Saviour".

Mary the mother of Jesus said "I am a sinner, this is God my Saviour". "There is born unto you this day in the city of David a Saviour which is Christ the Lord". Yes, Jesus was a good Man, but His goodness could not save us sinners. He was a moral Man but His morality could not save us sinners. He was a kind and gentle Man but His kindness and gentleness could not save us sinners. Only one thing could pay for sin, and that is the consequences of sin which is death, and Jesus died and took upon Himself the full penalty for your sins and for mine.

Now in the Book of the Acts chapter 4 and verse 12 we read: "Neither is there salvation in any other: for there is none other name under heaven given among men, whereby we must be saved". Yes, if we are going to be saved there is no other name under heaven, whereby we must be saved". The next time you utter the word Jesus, my friend; the next time you hear someone sing about Jesus; the next time we open our Hymn Books and sing about Jesus remember that Name means Saviour.

Some years ago I went into a barber's shop in a town where I had never been before, (I was there for a week of meetings). I walked into his shop and I was not in the chair many minutes until the barber began to use bad language. I could tolerate that for a little bit until he began to take the name of Jesus Christ in vain, and I could not take that. I stopped and I said, "Excuse me, sir, but you have spoken unkindly of a very dear Friend of mine". He said, "I do not know any friend you have, I have never seen them before". I said, "Oh, yes, I have a dear Friend, His name is Jesus, and you have spoken badly about Him. I do not appreciate that". He did not like my reaction to his language, but before I left that shop he knew that Jesus Christ did something for him. You cannot treat that Name lightly, my friend, and do not ever take it in vain, and do not ever use it blasphemously. "Thou shalt call His name Jesus, for He shall save His people from their sins".

How does Jesus Christ go about saving us? He had to take upon Himself the penalty of our sin, not part of it but the full penalty. Romans chapter 6, verse 23 says, "For the wages of sin is death", and the only way Christ could deal with our sins was to take our place and take on Him our sins, not in Him, there was no sin in Him but He took upon Him your sins and my sins, and when Jesus Christ died He died on that cross for you and for me. We have to recognise that, we have to apprehend that, we have to understand that. Do you apprehend what salvation is? It is rescuing, delivering someone from the penalty and guilt of sin. Do you apprehend that? Do you understand that? That is as simply as I can say it, dear friends, but you do not stop at apprehending it, you have to appropriate it, you have to say 'Yes, minister, I believe you are right, I am a sinner, and I do believe that

Jesus Christ the Son of God died on that Cross for my sins. That is apprehending it, and that is the first step in appropriating it.

Now we come to the means of this salvation from a doctrinal viewpoint. Turn to the third chapter of the Gospel according to John. In John chapter three we have the story of salvation in terms of a doctrinal word 'regeneration'. Generation, of course, means the beginning. You have a generator in your automobile, and that is how you start your car. When the generator dies you do not go. You get a rebuilt generator or a new generator or a new car. Generate is to start. Adam was generated by God: God created Adam, and Adam wilfully, and knowingly, and intentionally and deliberately disobeyed God, and when he did he died spiritually. Now the wages of sin is death. Adam is now degenerated. He was generated, he got a start, now he is degenerated. God gave him life, now he is spiritually dead. God said, "Adam, in the day you eat that forbidden fruit, you will surely die", and die he did. Now, all the offspring of Adam came into the world spiritually dead: Romans 5, verse 12: "For by one man, Adam, sin entered into the world, and death by sin; and so then death passed upon all men, for that all have sinned". God wants all to be saved. God did His part.

Someone said, not along ago at a Bible conference, and they were sincere, "By grace are we saved plus nothing". I said, "I am sorry I have to disagree with that, that is not totally scriptural". He said, "Oh, yes it is". "No it is not, that is half the truth, but half the truth could lead people in darkness" "For by grace are ye saved, through faith" By grace, through faith, plus nothing. Yes, God's grace makes it possible, but you are going to have to receive it by faith, and so am I or we will never be saved. Salvation is by grace: God's part, "through faith": our part plus nothing. Now, God did His part, what must I do to fulfill my part?

In Acts chapter 16 and verse 31 Paul and Silas were in prison; they were paying a price for a sin they never committed; they were simply preaching the Gospel; they were thrown into prison, and there was an earthquake which disturbed the jailer, and he let out with a cry: "What must I do to be saved?". Paul and Silas answered that cry, and they said: "Believe on the Lord Jesus Christ and thou shalt be saved". Man's part is simply by faith to believe that Jesus Christ the Son of God is the Saviour of the world, but you will never be saved nor will I until we appropriate what we apprehend. We know we are sinners, we know Jesus came and died on a cross. Everybody in the world knows that. 'There was a man by the name of Jesus who was crucified on a cross', but that I must appropriate; "The Son of God loved me, and gave Himself for me," and that must come to you in experience. We must not only apprehend but appropriate this great salvation.

If I appropriate by faith the death of Christ, can I be sure that I will be saved? Is there any assurance that my asking God to save me He will save me? Well, what does the Bible say? The one text I gave you in Acts 16:31: "Believe on the Lord Jesus Christ, and thou shalt be saved". Or Acts 4:12: "Neither is there salvation in any other, for there is none other name under heaven given among men whereby we must be saved", or Romans 10:13: "Whosoever shall call upon the Name of the Lord shall be saved".

Suppose there could be one person in the audience, who acknowledges that he or she is a sinner, they have no problem with that, they understand that, and now want to leave this building saved, knowing if they die unsaved they are going to hell forever and they do not want that, and, tonight, in all sincerity they lift their heart in a silent prayer, no one but God will hear it because it will not be uttered audibly, they say, "Lord, I am a sinner, please save me." I guarantee you, on the authority of the Word of God, you will walk out of this building S-A-V-E-D- saved. How do I know that? That is what God says in His Word: "Whosoever shall call upon the Name of the Lord shall be saved".

There is a process or a further means explained in doctrinal terms. One is John chapter 3, it is called the new birth or regeneration. When one gets saved, he is born again, he is regenerated. Every unsaved person is degenerated: spiritually dead, so the Word of God declares.

Now you want new life, you do not want to end up in eternity spiritually dead, separated from God, you want eternal life, so you ask God to save you,

In the Gospel according to John there are series of sevens. In the first chapter there are *seven descriptions of Deity*, seven descriptions of the Lord Jesus Christ. Then there are *seven declarations of Diety*, seven times the Lord said, "I am". There are also *demonstrations of Deity* in the seven miracles that Christ performed before His death on the cross.

Also in John's Gospel there are seven demands from Deity. One of them is in chapter 3; *they are the seven musts in the Gospel according to John.* Let us look at a couple of these. I am reading from verse 1. "There was a man of the Pharisees, named Nicodemus, a ruler of the Jews: The same came to Jesus by night, and said unto Him, Rabbi, (or 'Teacher') we know that Thou art a Teacher come from God: for no man can do these miracles that Thou doest, except God be with him. Jesus answered and said unto him, Verily, verily (you can translate this, 'Truly, truly, or 'Amen, amen', any of these will fit the Greek text) Verily, verily, I say unto thee, Except a man be born again,(except ye be regenerated. He is now spiritually dead, you cannot enter into heaven spiritually dead) except a man be born again, he cannot see the kingdom of God". Now there are two half questions in the context. Number one, Verse 4: "Nicodemus said unto Him, How can a man be born when he is old? can he enter the second time into his mother's womb, and be born?" You say, 'That is a stupid question'. Now suppose, dear Christian brothers and sisters, someone were to say to you, "Do you go to that church where they preach that 'born again' stuff?" You say, "Yes, I do". They say, "What do they mean by that?" Could you explain to an unsaved person what it means to be born again?

Do not be so hard on Nicodemus, go easy on him. What does it mean to be born again? "How can a man be born when he is old? can he enter the second time into his mother's womb, and be born?" "Jesus answered, Verily, verily, (Truly, truly, Amen, Amen), I say unto thee, Except a man be born of water and of the Spirit, he cannot enter into the kingdom of God". Now suppose it were possible for one to enter into the mother's womb, and be born the second time, if that were possible, the second birth would not be any better than the first birth, it would still be a physical birth, so you read in verse 6: "That which is born of the flesh is flesh" Watch closely your Bible: "That which is born of the Spirit is spirit". Two different words for spirit. Do you see one with the capital 'S' and the other with a small 's', do you see that? That which is born of the Holy Spirit is the human spirit . This is a spiritual regeneration. Because we are spiritually dead we need spiritual life.

Here is the first 'must': "Marvel not that I said unto thee, Ye must be born again". Why must we be born again? Because we were not born right the first time: Psalm 51:5, "We were born in sin, and shapen in iniquity". "All have sinned". We need a new birth, dear friends.

The word again in the English Bible is literally translated 'from above'. If you have a marginal Bible you have a number or a letter beside the word again; look over at the margin and you will see in your margin *from above*. You see, this is not a natural birth; it can not be provided on planet earth; it is a birth that comes from above, it comes from God, it is the new birth -the regeneration. Now, we have the 'must' of the new birth. Let us look at the mystery of the new birth. Verse 8: "The wind bloweth where it listeth, and thou hearest the sound thereof, but canst not tell whence it cometh, and whither it goeth". The wind blows, you do not know where it is coming from, and you do not know where it is going. There is an enigma about the wind. One of the reasons why your weatherman cannot predict accurately the weather is because he cannot control an instant shift of the wind; he could give you a prediction and within ten minutes the winds could shift and change completely his prediction.

Some years ago I was in Minnesota, and each evening when I would go to my room there was some news on the television. There were three men and they had a good time, they had a good clean sense of humour; their news programme was really entertaining. There was the anchor man, and then the sportscaster, and the weatherman. One evening while listening to the news, after I had finished my ministry that night, the weatherman gave his report, and after he gave a long talk about the weather and pointed to the maps, he said, "Well, folks, the conclusion is, tomorrow will be fair and warmer". Well, we woke up the next morning to eight inches of snow in Minnesota. I could not wait until that night, I wanted to know how the anchor man and the sportscaster was going to get after old George the weatherman. They started out that night: The anchor man said to the sportscaster, "You will never guess what I did this morning" The sportscaster said, "What did you do?". He said, "I shoveled off eight inches of fair and warmer" What happened? Why did the weatherman miss it? He could not control the winds. There is an enigma about the wind, and your weatherman cannot always predict with accuracy.

The Lord Jesus said, 'There is a mystery about this new birth. The wind blows where it will, thou hearest the sound thereof, but you can't tell where it comes from, and whither it goeth: so is every one that is born of the Spirit". That is called in the Bible 'born again'. "Except a man be born again". *The doctrine is regeneration.* Now this is how we get salvation: we are born again, we call on the Lord and ask Him to save us, because we know we are lost.

The question is, How can I be sure that I am saved? Number one, I just take God at His Word: "For whosoever shall call upon the Name of the Lord shall be saved". *Number two, I'll tell you, the second way I knew that I was saved in* 1927, *I was a different person,* I received a new nature, I was far, far from being perfect as I am still, but I knew something happened within me: the Holy Spirit of God witnessed with my human spirit that I was a child of God. *I knew I was saved for three reasons, one, the Bible told me so, two, the Holy Spirit witnessed within me, and, three, I was not the same person that I was before I was born again.* I noticed something, and you know, my parents began to notice it.

My mother said, "Son, you are different" I said, "Yes, mother, I have been saved". My mother was the first person I led to Christ, she did not know what happened to me, I knew something happened, and my mother knew something had happened in her teenage son.

You have the manifestations of the new life. Have you had a change? Have you been born again? Now, if you have you may wonder, "Well, can I ever lose this salvation?". I will tell you whether you can or not. In just dealing with this one doctrine, are you ready for this? If anyone can tell me how a person who has been born can be unborn, then you have the answer to whether you can lose this salvation or not. Anyone who wants to try for that, I will sit down and talk with you. You tell me how a person who has been born can be unborn. No way! My fellowship with God can be broken, but my relationship cannot be, because I am now God's child by birth. I have been born into the family of God, I have salvation, can I ever lose it? If I could ever be unborn I could lose it. Tell me, I will be glad to talk to you about how a born person can ever be unborn, I would like to know. The reason why I am saying this is because the life that God gave to you when you were born again is His own life: "I give unto them eternal, everlasting life; they shall never perish". John chapter 10, verse 28.

Is that plain? Do you need to go to a university to get the sense of that? There is a promise: "I give unto them eternal life", and with that promise there is a pledge: "they shall never perish". Who said so? The Lord Jesus said so. "My Father who gave them to me is greater than I. No man can pluck them out of My Father's hand". Who said that? Jesus said that. A person born again can never, ever, ever be unborn. Fellowship can be broken but not a relationship. My daddy was rather strict with us boys; there were six of us. He was an immigrant from Germany, and life in Germany was different away back in those days, and that is a long time ago. In America if you wanted to discuss time you say, "That happened away back when Pike's Peak was still a pimple", So that means it is a long, long time ago. Dad came from Germany, and he had some lifestyles that we did not understand in America, and we learned some wonderful lessons from dad, and if we were real bad dad would punish us. Now dad never had to do this with me, but a neighbour had to do it with their boy Jimmy. Jimmy was a bad, bad boy, and Jimmy's father said to him, "Now, Jim you are hurting your mother; you have changed your behaviour, I am going to have to deal with you", But Jim who lived two doors from us did not change his behaviour, and one day his daddy said, "Now look Jim, you are breaking your mother's heart, either shape up or ship out, you will no longer stay in this house and break your mother's heart. Make up your mind, shape up or ship out". Well, Jim worked hard at shaping up, and one day he shipped out. His fellowship with his father was broken but he could not break the relationship, even if he changed his name his father was still his father. The fellowship was broken but the relationship could never be broken. He came from his father's loins. No way could he break the relationship, even if he changed his name legally he is still the son of Mr. Stewart.

Dear friends, once you have salvation it is impossible to be unborn; God has given to you eternal life. This life is God's own life, and with the gift there is a guarantee: you will never, not ever perish. Read the tenth chapter of the Gospel according to John.

I could give you some more doctrines, but I am going to give you just one more. These are all under the umbrella of salvation: The doctrine of regeneration is under the umbrella of salvation. Turn to Romans chapter 5. Now we looked at the doctrine of regeneration -the new birth. If you have been born you can't be unborn, your fellowship with God can be broken but your relationship cannot be broken. You are God's child by birth, you have God's nature, you cannot be unborn. *Now let us look at the doctrine of justification*, see how that stacks up with the gift of salvation: Romans chapter 5, "Therefore being justified by faith". Now regeneration is the sovereign act of God whereby He imparts new life to a spiritually dead person. That life is God's own life, so that the spiritually dead person becomes a partaker of God's life - God's nature, born again, a new beginning of regeneration. Now let us look at this doctrine of justification; that is one of the words of the Gospel that comes under the umbrella of salvation: "Therefore being (or having been) justified by faith, we have peace with God through our Lord Jesus Christ".

Now a saved person has not only been regenerated or born again, but a saved person has been justified. Justification is the sovereign act of God, whereby He (God) declares righteous that sinner who comes to Him through faith in His Son the Lord Jesus Christ. Only God can justify a man. No man can justify another man. If I sin you can't justify me, you could forgive me for my sin but you can't justify me. How can you declare me right when you know I am wrong. Only God can declare righteous a hell-deserving sinner. It is the doctrine of justification: the sovereign act of God, whereby He declares righteous. It is a judicial term, a courtroom term. He does not make us righteous, He imputes to us the righteousness of His Son, while He has imputed to His Son your sins and my sins. This is God's plan for our salvation.

Now let me give it to you again. Justification is the sovereign act of God,whereby God declares righteous.

On Christmas Day 1927 I came to God, a teenager, I knew I was a sinner, and I asked God to save me. On that day in 1927 God justified me; He declared me righteous. I was no more justified Christmas Day 1927 than I am today, and I am no less justified now than I was in 1927. God cannot change. God made the declaration. God declared you righteous. Do you know anywhere in the Bible where God can reverse His decision and take from you that which He has given you as a gift? How can God now declare you unrighteous? You say, "As a Christian I might sin". Not only you might sin, you have sinned. There is not a Christian in this room who could say, "I have not sinned since I have been saved". If you were to say that you would commit a sin now by lying. Every Christian has sinned. You never lost your salvation, my friend, when you sinned. Your fellowship with God was broken, you could not read your

Bible and get sense out of it; you could not pray; you could not testify to a lost sinner; you are out of fellowship with God, but your relationship to God cannot be changed, because you can't be unborn, and God cannot unjustify those whom He has justified. That is God's Word. Only God can justify a person.

We had an experience in the sporting world in America: There was a baseball player who was possibly one of the best baseball players in the history of baseball in America; he is a young man not known any more; his name was Pete Rose, and Pete Rose was one of the most exciting baseball players who ever played the game. Pete Rose got involved in a scandal - a gambling scandal which is illegal; no professionsal sports person can ever wager money on a game in which he or she is involved. Pete Rose got involved in a gambling scandal; he was brought before the Judge. and I witnessed the trial on television, and as Pete Rose stood before the Judge, that Judge said: "Pete Rose, you are one of the most exciting ballplayers I have ever watched; you are my favourite ballplayer". He said, "I can forgive you for what you did, but I cannot justify you, you did wrong, I must be an honest Judge, I now sentence you to prison", And I saw the tears come from the eyes of that Judge when he said, "Pete, I love the way you play ball, I can forgive you but I cannot justify you, you did wrong, I cannot declare you right".

God only can declare a wrong person right, How? Because His Son took your wrong and my wrong upon Himself, and God imputed our sin to Jesus and imputed His righteousness to us. Can God reverse His gift? Can God change His mind? Can He now undeclare His judicial passing, "I now declare you righteous". God cannot do that. God is Immutable; He cannot change His mind.

Once I had it, I learned I could never lose it. Some folks do not like to hear that; they do not believe that the blood of Jesus Christ cleanseth them from all sin. They sing it but they do not believe it. They recite the twenty-third Psalm but they do not believe it: "'Though I walk through the valley of the shadow of death, I will fear no evil, for Thou art with me, And I will dwell in the House of the Lord (for how long?) Do not recite it if you do not believe it. Do not lie. Do not ever recite that you will dwell in the House of the Lord for ever, if you do not believe that Jesus died for all of your sins. Friends, He did not die just for some of them, if He did we are all as good as lost now. 1 John 1:7:"The blood of Jesus Christ, God's Son, cleanseth us from all sin". Salvation, what is it? How can I get it?

If I get it, will I know I have it? And if I have it, can I ever lose it?

I have sinned since 1927, I have never lost my salvation nor have you.

Read Hebrews chapter 6. If you can lose your salvation, you could never get it back again according to the Word of God. When your fellowship is broken, keep your confessions up to date; stay in fellowship with God, you will always have the peace,and the joy and the assurance of your salvation!

AMEN AND AMEN!

The All of God's Sovereignty

---------------------------------- ❖ ----------------------------------

I would like to continue a very easy subject to understand, based on the most inclusive word in all
languages: the little word 'All' - A-L-L, we are going to
follow through in our study . We began dealing with the
'All' of Scripture: 11 Timothy 3:16, "All Scripture is given by
inspiration of God", Then we looked at the 'All' of sin, "All
have sinned, and come short of the glory of God". (Romans
3:23). We went on to study the 'All' of Christ (Colossians 3:
9). Then we spent some time in the 'All' of salvation, "God
is not willing that any should perish, but that all should
come to repentance".

Now we want to study the 'All' of the sovereignty of
God. Open your Bible, please, to the epistle of Romans
chapter 8. There are two texts which I want to use. One is
Romans chapter 8, the very familiar twenty-eighth verse,
and then we will turn to the Gospel according to Matthew,

chapter 19. In Romans chapter 8, verse 28, a very familiar text, I am sure many of you have memorised it: "And we know that all things (not a few things, not some things, not many things, not most things, all things) work together for good to them that love God" (Not those whom God loves, those who love Him) "to them that are the called according to His purpose". A great text, do not read something into it that is not there, and, please, do not leave anything out that is in there. Having drawn your attention to this text, go back with me, please, to the Gospel according to Matthew chapter 19, and there is another verse that we should look at and that is verse 26: "Jesus beheld them, and said unto them, With men this is impossible; (Here is a very important 'All') but with God all things are possible". Now, if you are a Christian you believe what that verse says. Negatively in another passage it says, "Nothing is impossible with God". The positive verse: "With God all things are possible".

Recently I picked up a biography on the late William McKendrick, a Scottish preacher, I heard him in 1930 in Philadelphia, Pennsylvania, and in his subject he did not use the word 'Sovereignty' but he chose the little word 'Able', *and he had picked out about six texts which tells us that God is able to do something: He is able to save to the uttermost. He is able to succour. He is able to keep that which I have committed unto Him*, and at the end of each one of the preacher's explanation of that text he made the statement: "The ability of God knows no inability". Not once did he use the word 'Sovereignty of God', but in substance that is what he was saying: "The ability of God knows no inability".

"With God all things are possible".

The words 'Sovereign' and 'Sovereignty' do not appear in our King James Bible. You will find it in one or two modern translations; it really comes to us from the Latin 'Super', and that which is 'Super' is unequalled and unexcelled. You pick up your newspaper or watch your television and they are advertising sales in the market place, and someone will come through with a super sale. Do not believe it. A super sale is a sale that is unequal; it has never been equaled and never will be equaled. A super sale: that is the superlative, the super, you can't get any higher than that. *To say that God is sovereign is to say that God is the super-power of the world*; of all time and eternity. God is the super-power, unequalled and unexcelled. *To say that God is sovereign is to say that God is eternal*: He never had a beginning, He will never have an ending. *To say that God is sovereign is to say that He is self-contained*; He does not need anyone to assist Him in anything. *To say that God is sovereign is to say that God does whatever He chooses to do*, whenever He chooses to do it, wherever He chooses to do it, involving whomsoever He chooses to involve: you, your loved ones, me, my loved ones, yes, God is sovereign. That is the kind of a God we Christians worship, that is the God of the Bible, that is God and the Father of our Lord Jesus Christ. At no time can any power say: 'Step aside, God, I am taking over', it is impossible, He is the sovereign God - the super-power of all time and through eternity.

I am going to take you back to Genesis chapter 18, I would like to use this passage to prepare us for the rest of the lesson. In Genesis chapter 18 God took Abraham into His confidence: God is going to destroy some cities. The reason for God's decision to destroy the citiesis that they were the breeding place of a sin that God hates and judges, the sin of homosexuality. God took Abraham into His confidence to tell him He was going to destroy those cities. Now, Abraham had some kinfolk in one of those cities, and he knew his kinfolk were not homosexuals, and he begins to plead with God, and in this chapter you will find one of the great intercessory prayers of the Old Testament. Abraham begins to plead with God: "Lord, if there are fifty righteous people in the city will you destroy it? or forty-five, or forty, or thirty, or twenty". He is appealing to God with a heart of compassion and intercessory prayer. When we come to verse 25 of this chapter you will see a tremendous discovery that Abraham made in contact with God. It is in the form of a question, but it is the kind of a question that contains the answer. Here is the question: "Shall not the Judge of all the earth do right?" You have the answer to that question. If you know God you know He always does right. If God could do wrong once He would cease to be God. Rightness, righteousness is one of the essential attributes of Deity without which God could not be God. "Shall not the Judge of all the earth do right?" Quite a text for a man with a heavy heart for loved ones in a city that is about to be destroyed because of wickedness, and knowing that your loved ones are not involved in that sin.

Turn to the Book of Exodus, we are going to look at a key chapter that might be mind-boggling to some of us, but may I remind you that this has always been in your Bible, and if this stirs you up it is because you missed it, it has always been there. In Exodus chapter 4 God is seeking a man to lead His people out of the bondage of Egypt, but more than that, to speak for God. 'I want a spokesman, and I want a leader', God called upon Moses. Beginning with verse 10 we have the excuse of Moses why he feels he does not qualify to answer this call from God. I am reading from Exodus chapter 4, verse 10: "And Moses said unto the LORD, O my Lord, I am not eloquent, neither heretofore, nor since Thou hast spoken unto Thy servant: but I am slow of speech, and of a slow tongue". Watch carefully what follows: God is speaking, "And the LORD said unto him, Who hath made man's mouth?" You have the answer to that, God, of course, created man. "who maketh the dumb, or deaf?" The answer is in the question God is speaking. God is saying "I am responsible". Let me ask you a simple question, Do you believe that God could bring every baby into this world capable of speaking if the baby should live long enough and learn, do you believe God could do that? Do you believe He could? Why, of course, you do. God could bring every baby into the world to speak. Do you believe God could bring every baby into this world with sound hearing? Of course you do or you would not be here. Every baby is not born into this world with the ability to speak or to hear, and God is saying here, I take full responsibility. That is exactly what He is saying. Moses said, "Lord, I can't speak for you"

Who do you think controls the children coming into this world? "I take full responsibility." That is what God is saying. He deals further in verse 11: "Who hath made man's mouth? or who maketh the dumb or the deaf, or the seeing, or the blind?" God said, "Have not I the LORD". A baby is born into the world blind and who will never see. God said I take full responsibility. He is saying, I could bring every baby into the world with twenty-twenty vision, but it does not happen that way and I take full responsibility.

Dear friends, what you see in this text is the sovereignty of God. God is capable of bringing every child into this world with good vision and good hearing, and He said, "I the Lord have not done it". The sovereignty of God. God does whatever He chooses to do, whenever He chooses to do it, wherever He chooses to do it, involving whomsoever He chooses to involve. It could be you, your loved one, me or my loved one, and God is always right. If God could be wrong once He would cease to be God.

This is a truth on the sovereignty of God.

Turn to Amos, one of the minor prophets. Each of the minor prophets have a major message; they are not minor in significance but, rather, minor in size when compared with the larger prophecies of Isaiah, Jeremiah or Ezekiel. I want to read from chapter 3: "Hear this Word that the LORD hath spoken against you, O children of Israel, against the whole family which I brought up from the land of Egypt, saying, You only have I known of all the families of the earth: therefore I will punish you for all your iniquities" This is the first of a series of questions. I will read the first one and go to the last one to save a little time. Verse 3: "Can two walk together, except they be agreed?" Can two walk together except by previous appointment? We are going on to the last of the questions:

Verse 6: "Shall there be evil in a city, and the LORD hath not done it?" Look at the question, what is the answer? God is speaking. This is not moral evil, Amos will explain the evil. God is not the author of evil.

In the epistle of James we are warned, Do not ever charge God with temptation, "God cannot be tempted with evil, neither tempteth He any man." This is not moral evil, God is not the author of sin. What is this evil? Amos is going to explain it for us. Move to chapter 4, God is speaking, notice the first person, singular in your Bible, I am reading from verse 6 which begins a new paragraph. God said, "I also have given you cleanness of teeth in all your cities, and want of bread in all your places". That is a famine, want of bread, there was no need to brush your teeth because you had no food. God said, I did it. I gave it to you.

There was a reason why God sent the famine to His people, "yet have ye not returned unto me, saith the LORD". God loves His people, He wants them to be in fellowship with Him, and when we drift, God seeks to bring us back, and sometimes He has to use measures that are very difficult for us. God said, I sent the famine, but you did not return unto me. Verse 7, Notice the first Person singular, God is speaking, Amos is writing God's message, "And also I have withholden the rain from you, when there were yet three months to the harvest: and I caused it to rain upon one city, and caused it not to rain upon another city". God said, When it rains, I cause the rain; when there is no rain I am responsible for it.

God controls what God creates. The sovereignty of God!

We complain about the weather. Pretty difficult to be satisfied with the weather: some like it hot, some like it cold, some like it wet, some like it dry. God says, This is my hand. When there is a drought that is one of the evils. When there is too much rain and there is flood-damage, God said, I did it. The sovereignty of God! God is behind the scenes controlling the scenes: He is behind everything.

Read verse 8, Amos chapter 4: "So two or three cities wandered unto one city, to drink water; but they were not satisfied: yet have ye not returned unto Me, saith the LORD." Here is the sovereignty of God as plain as you will ever see it: look at verse 9, "I" said God "have smitten you with blasting and mildew: when your gardens and your vineyards and your fig trees and your olive trees increased, the palmerworm devoured them". The plague of grasshoppers came in when it was right for harvest and they devoured all the vegetation, God said, I did it, I create the grasshopper, I control the grasshopper. God said, I take full responsibility for that plague of grasshoppers. The sovereignty of God! These things happen, they are bad things, they happen to good people, to God's people, and yet He said, "Ye have not returned unto me, saith the LORD".

Look at verse 10, God speaks again, Amos merely writes the words of God. I believe in the verbal inspiration of the Bible, God gave every word in the original manuscripts. Verse 10: "I have sent among you the pestilence after the manner of Egypt: your young men have I slain with the sword". The Egyptian bondage God could have prevented. The Babylonian captivity God could have prevented. Many were slain, and the nation was taken into bondage, God said, I did it. As a matter of fact He told Jeremiah in advance He was going to do it. People were wandering from Him, and we read, "yet have ye not returned unto me, saith the LORD".

Verse 11, to go back to our introductory comments; "I have overthrown some of you, as God overthrew Sodom and Gomorrah, and ye were as a firebrand plucked out of the burning: yet have ye not returned unto me, saith the LORD". God said, I did it. You can't read anything into that passage but the sovereignty of God. God said, I take full responsibility. What God creates God controls, whether animal life, anything that we call nature, that is God's natural creation, He is behind the scenes controlling the scenes. So when the weather does not suit you, just leave it with the Lord, He knows all about it, He takes full responsibility.

I would like you to turn to the New Testament and the Book of the Acts: we are going to look at the chapter that records the conversion of Saul of Tarsus. Acts chapter 9, verse 1: "And Saul, yet breathing out threatenings and slaughter against the disciples of the Lord, went unto the high priest, And desired of him letters to Damascus to the synagogues, that if he found any of this way, whether they were men or women, he might bring them bound unto Jerusalem.

And as he journeyed, he came near Damascus: and suddenly there shined round about him a light from Heaven: And he fell to the earth, and heard a voice saying unto him, Saul, Saul, why persecutest thou me? And he said, Who art Thou, Lord? And the Lord said, I am Jesus whom thou persecutest: it is hard for thee to kick against the pricks.

I believe, although you may not agree with this, that this was his experience of salvation: the conversion of Saul of Tarsus, this is the record of his conversion. This is the day he was saved, "And he trembling and astonished (verse 6) said, Lord, (Watch the question from this new convert) what wilt Thou have me to do?" By the way, beloved friends, how long have you been saved? Have you yet asked God why He saved you, what He wants you to do with your life? Sometimes I wonder how many professing Christians have yet to say, "Lord, what do you want me to do?". What a question, on the day that a man gets converted!

Also, in the same chapter, the Lord sent a messenger to the street where Saul was and He said he has just asked me a question, and I want you to convey My answer. We are still in Acts chapter 9, reading from verse 13: "Ananias answered, Lord, I have heard by many of this man, how much evil he hath done to thy saints at Jerusalem: And here he hath authority from the chief priests to bind all that call upon Thy name".(Watch verse 15, this has always been in your Bible) "But the Lord said unto him, Go thy way: for he is ('this little Jew that I have just saved') a chosen vessel unto me, to bear my name before the Gentiles, and kings, and the children of Israel" Watch verse 16: "I will shew him (saith the Lord) how great things he must suffer for my name's sake".

Suppose the day you and I got saved we got a message from God, and He said, "I have saved you to suffer for my name's sake". He knew He could trust this man. How would you and I respond? We were so sure of our salvation the day we got saved, would we be just as sure of a message from God if He said, I saved you to suffer for my name's sake. The sovereignty of God! God does whatever He chooses to do, where, whenever, involving whomsoever. Yes, it could be you, your loved ones, me, my loved ones, God is always right!

When you read the autobiography of Paul in the Corinthians he lists some events - imprisonment, beaten, hated, despised. Yes he suffered, I believe possibly as much as any man or woman, apart from the Lord Jesus Christ. God said, That is why I saved you. We may not understand all that God says; we may not always trace Him, but, beloved, we must always trust Him. God is always right!

Turn back to the Gospel according to John, and look at chapter 5: "After this there was a feast of the Jews; and Jesus went up to Jerusalem. Now there is at Jerusalem by the sheep market a pool, which is called in the Hebrew tongue Bethesda, having five porches. In these lay a great multitude of impotent folk, of blind, halt, withered, waiting for the moving of the water. For an angel went down at a certain season into the pool, and troubled the water: whosoever then first after the troubling of the water stepped in was made whole of whatsoever disease he had. And a certain man was there, which had an infirmity thirty and eight years. When Jesus saw him lie, and knew that he had been now a long time in that case, He saith unto him, Wilt thou be made whole? The impotent man answered him, Sir, I have no man, when the water is troubled, to put me into the pool: but while I am coming, another steppeth down before me. Jesus saith unto him, Rise, take up thy bed, and walk. And immediately the man was made whole, and took up his bed, and walked: and on the same day was the sabbath"

When I first read that passage as a young Christian I said to myself: There was a great multitude of people who needed attention; they had affliction; they all were there to be healed, and here comes God Himself in the Person of His Son, and He heals one, and walks by all the rest. I can't always understand my Lord, but I can trust Him. He always does right. Could Christ have healed all of that great multitude? Of course He could have but He did not, He is sovereign, He does whatever He chooses to do, whether, wherever, involving whomsoever, and, beloved, we must believe that He is always right. I cannot understand all the works of my Lord but I trust Him.

In this Book we are introduced to a number of things about Job. *First of all God testifies to Job's faith*: God said, "... that man was perfect and upright, and one that feared God, and eschewed evil." (Job 1: 1). That is God's own testimony of Job: his faith.

Then we have a testimony of his family: how large his family was, and the writer tells us of his sons and daughters. After we have a testimony of his faith and of his family we have a *testimony of his fortune*: he was one of the wealthiest men of his day. Then we have a *testimony of his fame*: he was one of the most famous men of his day. When you come to that first chapter and second chapter in Job something happens: Thieves come in and begin to steal his livestock, and one by one he loses his fortune. Then a cyclone strikes, and his children are killed, he lost his family. Then he himself was stricken with a disease that isolated him from all society. The historians tell us it was the worst form of leprosy or cancer that a human being could contract. As a matter of fact under the Mosaic Law anyone with leprosy walking down the roadway must cup his hands and cry three times, "Unclean, unclean, unclean!" he was isolated from society, no one could affiliate with him, it was a contagious disease. When you come to the second chapter of Job he is sitting on an ash heap out on the city dump, no longer capable of affiliating with the rest of society. He lost his family. He lost his fortune and he lost his fame, And when you come to the thirteenth chapter you hear him say: "Though He slay me, yet will I trust in Him"(Verse 15).

Do you trust God? Do you trust God? Proverbs chapter 3, verses 5 and 6: "Trust in the LORD with all thine heart" Not a half-hearted trust, "Trust in the LORD with all thine heart; and lean not unto thine own understanding. In all thy ways acknowledge Him, and He shall direct thy paths".

1 Peter 5:7, "Casting all your care upon Him; for He careth for you".

Do we really trust God? "We know that all things work together for good to them that love God" (Romans 8:28).

When you go back to the Book of Job read the last chapters and there you will find the glorious climax: God gave Job more after the trial than he had before, and he learned the truth of Romans 8:28 that 'all things', the bad things, the difficult things, they are working together for good to them that love God, Not those whom God loves, God loves everyone in this audience, but do we all love Him? If we love Him He said, 'you will keep my commandments'. To trust God is to obey God.

I do not speak very often of some valleys the Lord has put me through. My first wife was stricken and left totally paralysed. For seven years God put me in a school - a school of learning. I learned to bathe her, clothe her, to provide her food, to take her wherever I went, in a wheelchair. Then God allowed an affliction to come to my eldest son. I watched him die for five years. Three years ago he died at age sixty. A trial! You can trust me when I tell you: I am looking back to those valley experiences and I know that they all worked together for good as I trusted God. Do you trust Him? You can trust Him; He is always right; never wrong. Now, with God all things are possible. That is His sovereignty. I believe in the sovereignty of God, and I believe that everything that God allows, and everything that God sends He has behind it His purpose. Watch the last word in Romans 8:28: "and we know that all things work together for good to them that love God, to them who are the called according to His purpose". Ah, beloved, God has a purpose for what comes into my life. He may not show me while I am going through the trial, but if I trust Him I can look back and I can say, I know that "all things work together for good to them that love Him, to them who are the called according to His purpose". I cannot tell you how all things work together for good. I would like to be able to tell you how. I cannot tell you how but I can tell you on the authority of God's Word, and from my own experience. I cannot tell you how, but I can tell you that they do work together for good. I will not exchange one valley experience in my life for the blessings that have come to me as I walk from day to day learning. Those trials were a school of experience: I had not been there before: I had never been through it before. This is something new to me, a minister of God's Word, how will I handle it? I am not proud of my first reactions, but as I thought through the Scriptures and kept in fellowship with God He gave me peace, and I am looking back and I am telling you that all things do work together for good to those who love Him, and who are the called according to His purpose.

We have looked at two 'Alls'; the 'ALL' of the sovereignty of God, and truth that 'ALL' things- good things, bad things, 'ALL' things work together for good to those who love Him and who are the called according to His purpose.

Our next lesson is the last, and it might be nice for all of us to close with the blessing of Philippians 4:19: "And my God shall supply (what?) all your need".

There are needs here. Do not tell me you have not a need, I would not believe it. What is your need? We all have needs: "My God shall supply all your need!" The sovereignty of God in human suffering. Trust Him, beloved, He knows the end from the beginning, and one day you will see that all things did work together for good.

AMEN AND AMEN!

The All of God's Supply

❖

Turn to Philippians chapter 4. This series has been based upon the little word 'All': We began with 'All Scripture' 11. Timothy 3:16: "All Scripture is given by inspiration of God". We follow that up with the 'All' of sin: Romans 3:23: "For all have sinned and come short of the glory of God". Our next was the All of Christ: "Christ is all in all". Then we had a study on the 'All' of salvation: 11. Peter 3:9: "God is not willing that any should perish, but that all should come to repentance". Then we looked at the 'All' of the Sovereignty of God. Now we want to look at the 'All' of God's supply: Philippians 4:19 "But my God shall supply all your need according to His riches in glory by Christ Jesus".

This is one of the familiar texts among God's people, and I am sure that many can quote this text from memory:

"My God shall supply all your need according to His riches in glory by Christ Jesus" Do not claim that text before you examine its context. I want you to note those to whom Paul wrote these words: he said in the context here beginning with verse 13: "I can do all things through Christ which strengtheneth me. Notwithstanding ye (You Philippian Christians) have well done, that ye did communicate with my affliction". Paul suffered: as a matter of fact in Philippi he was in jail bound and bleeding for preaching the gospel, and he said, I have gone through some affliction, and ye Philippians have been kind to me. Verse 15: "Now ye Philippians know also, that in the beginning of the gospel, when I departed from Macedonia, no church communicated with me as concerning giving and receiving, but ye only." So you are the only church that considered my need, and I want you to know I appreciate that. Verse 16: "For even in Thessalonica ye sent once and again unto my necessity". He is commending the Philippian Christians for their sacrificial giving to the Lord's work; he is not bragging on them now, he is thanking God and thanking them. Verse 17: "Not because I desire a gift: but I desire fruit that may abound to your account". He said, verse 18: "But I have all, and abound: I am full, having received of Epaphroditus the things which were sent from you, an odour of a sweet smell, a sacrifice acceptable, well pleasing to God". That is quite a testimony with the saints in Philippi, is it not? Now watch; he is saying to a sacrificial people who were giving generously for the spread of the gospel: "My God shall supply all your need according to His riches in glory by Christ Jesus". Now, if I am a selfish Christian; self-centered; pitying myself; looking out for number one, I could not claim this verse. Fit in the context, beloved, it was addressed to people who gave sacrificially for the work of God and the spreading of the gospel, and Paul said to them, "My God shall supply all your need according to His riches in glory by Christ Jesus". Hopefully we can claim this verse, not simply because we memorised it and it is a familiar verse, but we have a claim upon God because we have been faithful in our Christian testimony; we have been faithful in our stewardship, and now we say "My God shall supply all my need".

Turn back to the Sermon on the Mount, and then we will return to Philippians chapter 4. In the Gospel according to Matthew there are some very important discourses. The Sermon on the Mount deals with the *principles of the Kingdom*. Chapter 13 in the Gospel according to Matthew deals with the *parables of the Kingdom*. Chapters 24 and 25 in Matthew deals with the *prophecies of the Kingdom*. This is a great book on the different topics that the Lord dealt with. The Sermon on the Mount: the principles of the Kingdom, how children of the King ought to live; how they ought to behave.

Look at chapter 6, verse 19: "Lay not up for yourselves treasures upon earth, where moth and rust doth corrupt, and where thieves break through and steal: But lay up for yourselves treasures in heaven, where neither moth nor rust doth corrupt, and where thieves do not break through nor steal: For where your treasure is, there will your heart be also". In other words, where your interest is, that is where your heart is. Very simple, very plain, very practical. Verse 22: "The light of the body is the eye: if therefore thine eye be single, thy whole body shall be full of light. But if thine eye be evil, (It all depends upon how we look upon life - a good eye or an evil eye, if we are out for selfish interests that is not good. If we lay up treasure in heaven that is good, that is a good eye) But if thine eye be evil thy whole body shall be full of darkness. If therefore the light that is in thee be darkness, how great is that darkness! No man can serve two masters: for either he will hate the one, and love the other; or else he will hold to the one, and despise the other. Ye cannot serve God and mammon". You cannot do it, no way!

Now He is going to encourage His disciples; He is going to use a statement: "Therefore, take no thought" (Verse 25), translated "Therefore, do not worry" "Therefore, take no thought for your life, what ye shall eat, or what ye shall drink". He is not saying you can be careless about your diet and eat too much food, or the wrong food. Do not worry about your food supply. Do not worry about it, take no thought about that, what ye shall eat, or what ye shall drink, nor yet for your body, what ye shall put on. Do not worry about your attire, whether you are in style or out of style, do not worry about that, take no thought concerning that. "Behold the fowls of the air: for they sow not, neither do they reap, nor gather into barns; yet your heavenly Father feedeth them" You see, God is a great supplier: He provides the food for the birds, but they have to go get it, do not forget that. He does not bring it to them, He provides it for them. He says, "Your heavenly Father feedeth them. Are ye not much better than they? Which of you by taking thought (Which of you by worrying) can add one cubit unto his stature? And why take ye thought for raiment? (Why do you worry about your wardrobe?) Consider the lilies of the field, how they grow; they toil not, neither do they spin: And yet I say unto you, That even Solomon in all his glory was not arrayed like one of these. Wherefore, if God so clothe the grass of the field, which to day is, and to morrow is cast into the oven, shall He not much more clothe you, O ye of little faith? Therefore take no thought, (Do not worry) saying, What shall we eat? or, What shall we drink? or, Wherewithal shall we be clothed? (For after all these things do the Gentiles (or, literally, the heathen) seek:) for your heavenly Father knoweth that ye have need of all these things. But seek ye first the kingdom of God, and His righteousness; and all these things shall be added unto you". What a text!

"Take therefore no thought for the morrow: for the morrow shall take thought for the things of itself. Sufficient unto the day is the evil thereof". That is a sermon in itself. A lot of practical teaching there. What does it tell us? Your Heavenly Father knows what you and I need. We do not have to tell Him what we need: He knows, He knows better than we do. Sometimes we think our greed is our need. Sometimes we translate our wants into what we would like to call our need. God knows what you need, and God knows what I need, and God is faithful and cares more about you and about me than we do about ourselves.

With this bit of background we are going back to Philippians chapter 4. We have talked a little bit about food, and clothing, raiment and the mundane things that money can buy, and after all, when most Christians quote Philippians 4:19 we think of material things - mundane things: the things that money can buy, but in the context of Philippians chapter 4, I want you to see, beloved, that there are some needs, (and I believe they are here tonight in an audience this size) that money cannot buy. Let us look at them, they fit into our lifestyle, let us learn that we have a God who can supply needs that money will never buy. Philippians chapter 4. We are going to keep verse 19 in the context, and we are going to see some needs that existed in the church in Philippi, and I think that these are needs that exist in many churches; many families: Money cannot buy these needs, but my God shall supply all your need.

Let us look at a few of them beginning with verse 1: "Therefore, my brethren, dearly beloved and longed for, my joy and crown, so stand fast in the Lord, my dearly beloved." Now he is going to speak to two women in the church in Philippi who were not getting along with each other; they just could not make it: Their names are rather different names, I do not know anybody named after these women: one is called Euodias (the 's' is silent. The late Dr. Ironside called her Odious, he tagged that on to her) "I beseech Euodias, and beseech Syntyche, (The late Dr. Ironside called the second one 'Soontouchy'). Here were two women Euodias and Syntyche: they were not getting along with each other, and Paul said, I beseech you two ladies that you be of the same mind in the Lord. Why do you not settle your difference? Why do you not bury the hatchet? and be of the same mind in the Lord.

Obviously there was a *need in the church in Philippi for harmony*, but you cannot buy harmony with money. I do not know, it is none of my business, but I would like to just wonder how many people in the audience, you came from your house to the meeting, but your house is not a home; it takes a heap of living to make a house a home, and you left to come to this service and harmony is lacking in your house? It is not a very healthy situation, is it? Isn't it sad when there is no harmony in the home; no harmony between husband and wife; lack of harmony between parents and children; lack of harmony among brothers and sisters; lack of harmony in the Assembly of God? You say, "Brother Strauss, are you speaking about Ireland?" I am speaking about human beings anywhere on planet earth.

Human nature is the same everywhere, dear friends. So many of us are so wrapped up with self, we are loaded with self-esteem, and we think of ourselves (and this is in Philippians) more highly than we ought to.

As soon as I become number one in my family there is lack of harmony. Do you need harmony dear friend? Has there been a rift, a division, a separation, you are really not on speaking terms. In the early days of my ministry I had a couple in the first church I pastored, and I heard a rumour about them. A member said, "Pastor, did you know that Mr. and Mrs. So and So do not speak to each other". I said, "Now are you sure that is so?" "Well, this is what I was told". "Now you better make sure, because I am going to visit this couple, and I may have to tell them where I heard this rumour" The person said, "Well, I am sure it is true, and I will tell you who told me". I made an appointment to visit this couple; they had two children, a son and a daughter, And I said, "I would like to come some evening and visit with you, and I would like to come after the children have been put to bed". They had no idea why I was coming. When I arrived, the children were in bed, and I sat on the sofa between them, and I said, "I heard a rumour that you do not speak to each other. Is that true or false?". The husband was silent, the wife, she said, "Yes, Pastor, that is true". I said, "How do you communicate?". She said, "Well, if my husband wants to tell me something he says to our son, 'You go tell that to your mother', and if I want to respond I go to my daughter and say, 'You go tell that to your father'". Ladies and gentlemen, for Christians that is a disgrace. I was young then, I am older now, I hope I have matured, but this is what I said to that couple: "You two ought to have your heads bashed together". I would not do it that way now, that was years ago, but I meant it when I said it. What a disgrace for Christian people who came to church every Sunday with their Bible, and bring their children to Sunday School, and the children never hear their parents talk to each other. Do you have some of that in your family; in your local Assembly; between employer and employee; between neighbours? Oh, dear Christian, my God shall supply all your need. Money won't buy it. You cannot buy harmony with money, but there is a God, He is your heavenly Father and He knows you and He knows me better than we know ourselves, and He wants us to know what kind of a Father He is. Do we know Him as the One who knows our need and who longs to meet our need?

Remember the context; Paul was writing to people who were on the giving end; who were sharing; who were kind to one another, and he said, "My God shall supply all your need". There was a lack of harmony in the church in Philippi. If there is a lack of harmony in lives my dear, dear friends my God shall supply all your need. Give Him a chance. Great is His faithfulness! The word 'faithful' is a verbal adjective which means 'reliable - dependable - trustworthy' To say that God is faithful is to say that you can count on God; you can depend on God, He is trustworthy, He is a right-eous God. Let us heal the lack of harmony! Money will never buy it, but, "My God shall supply all your need!"

Let us look again at the context of Philippians chapter 4. There was a need for harmony. Look at verse 4, "Rejoice in the Lord alway: and again I say, Rejoice". Now if you read through Paul's letter to the Philippians and count the number of times that you find the noun 'joy' and the verb 'rejoice', it will surprise you. Some commentators who have written books on Philippians, (in fact, I know three commentaries: where it is called the 'Epistle of Joy') they call it the 'Epistle of Joy'. Joy was lacking in the lives of the

Christians in Philippi. So much so that Paul gave them this statement. I want you to look at verse 4. What is the first word in that verse? 'Rejoice'. What is the last word in that verse? 'Rejoice'. That is a lot of stress on one subject in one short verse. "Rejoice in the Lord alway: and again I say, Rejoice". There was a need for happiness. Beloved, where there is no harmony there is no happiness. The joy goes out of the heart, the joy goes out of the home, the joy goes out of the ministry in the local assembly . Where there is no harmony there is no happiness. He said, "Rejoice in the Lord alway: and again I say, Rejoice".

I always enjoy passing out a little help to preachers and Sunday School teachers, and I always feel a sermon coming on with some verses, and this is one of those verses. Now watch this, the stress on rejoicing. "Rejoice in the Lord alway: and again I say, Rejoice". *He is stressing the need for joy.* Then, he gives to us the source of our rejoicing: "Rejoice in the Lord".

Do you know why there is a lack of harmony? Somebody is out of fellowship with God. When two are walking together in fellowship with God, they are walking together in fellowship with each other. Something is wrong with a relationship to Christ when Christians cannot live together in harmony. Our joy is in the Lord if we are in fellowship with Him and abiding in Him. *Then with that kind of harmony there is going to be happiness*; there is going to be joy.

Have you lost your joy? Be honest with yourself, be honest: Are you really a happy Christian? Can you sing the joyful songs of the Lord from your heart? You may have a terrible voice. I am no soloist but I can sing, O can I sing in the shower! Nobody hears me but God, I enjoy it, and I want to keep my heart happy, I do not want to lose my song.

When harmony goes out happiness goes out. Would you like to get your song back? There is a wonderful text: the last verse in Hebrews chapter 4, "Let us therefore come boldly unto the throne of grace, that we may obtain mercy, and find grace to help in time of need". You see, there is a throne in heaven, it is not a throne of judgment, one day it will be, it is still a throne of grace. In this dispensation of grace God's throne is a throne of grace, and He says, "Come boldly unto the throne of grace, that we may obtain mercy, and find grace to help in time of need". You say: "Brother Strauss, there is a need for harmony". Come to the throne of grace: take a fresh drink at the infinite, inexhaustible fountain of grace, and God will give you back your harmony. Have you lost your joy? Why don't you take it to the Lord: come boldly to the throne of grace, that ye may obtain mercy, and find grace to help in time of need. You say, "I have lost my joy". God wants to give it back to you. You can't buy it with money, but my God shall supply all your need. Do not leave here a miserable Christian who has lost his or her song.

I can't have too many more years to go at best, dear friends, but I want you to know, and I know the Lord hears me say this: I would rather die right now standing in this pulpit than live on to be a mean, grouchy, crotchety old man who can't get along with people. I would rather go to heaven a happy, joyful Christian in harmony with others. The throne of grace is still open, dear friends: "My God shall supply all your need" "Come boldly to the throne of grace".

Let us look at the context, and what else is in this fourth chapter? Well, *there was a need for harmony; there was a need for happiness, and there was a need for helpers*: see verse 3, "I entreat thee also, true yokefellow, help those women which laboured with me in the Gospel". The church needs some helpers; we need more helpers, dear friends: the local church needs them. We have sometimes more critics than helpers. In a huge football stadium back in our country they get a hundred thousand people; there are twenty two men on the field playing the game, and thousands of people telling them how they ought to do it; they are just looking on. Oh, they can tell those who are doing it how to do it, and sometimes the people who don't help are the most critical. Every church needs helpers, and every family needs helpers; every local assembly needs helpers. Paul said, Are you a helper? Are you willing to do what you are able to do? "My God shall supply all your need". Come to the fountain: God is waiting, He can supply all your need.

Let us look down in the context and see if there could be another need in the life of any one of us. This was a need in Philippi. I am reading verse 6: "Be careful (that is be anxious for nothing) for nothing; but in every thing by prayer and supplication with thanksgiving let your requests be made known unto God". Just tell it to the Lord. "My God shall supply all your need", Just tell it to Him. You say "He knows my need", but He wants you to trust Him; to rely on Him, not on money, not on influence but on Him. "My God shall supply all your need". Be a help, dear friends, there is a need for it in the family, help one another. I always try to advise married couples to help each other; just lend a helping hand: Ephesians 5:25 tells the husbands how to help their wives, and I just add something, it is not scriptural, I say to the men: "Do you want to be a helper with your wife? When your wife is making up the bed, make up the bed with her. When she is washing up the dishes, wash up the dishes with her, and if she is mopping up the floor, mop up the floor with her". Some of you got a bad idea there. We need helpers, do we not? Helpers in the home, helpers in our business, helpers in the church: "My God shall supply all your need". He can make a helper out of any one of us. Would you like to be a helper? "My God shall supply all your need".

Then looking down at the context we read, verse 8: "Finally, brethren, whatsoever things are true, *whatsoever things are honest*". Now, if there was not a need for honesty among some of the saints in Philippi why would Paul have written this? He was directed by the Spirit of God.

I ask myself, you ask yourself: "Am I a totally honest Christian? Am I trust worthy? Am I a Christian of integrity? Can I be depended upon? Do I speak the truth? There is a need for honesty among God's people. Integrity is lacking, dear friends, and I am sorry to tell you, (Do not tell me I don't know what I'm talking about. My sixty years, almost sixty-one years in the ministry in more than 2,000 churches.) integrity is lacking among too many of God's people: dishonest people, some come to church every Sunday, bring their Bible, go through the ritual.

I had a dentist back in Pennsylvania in the early Nineteen Forties; a good singer; a fine Christian. I went for dental work one day, and I said, "Would you come some Sunday night and sing for us?" He said, "Oh, thank you", he did not comply, and going back for some more dental work, I said, "You have not yet given me a date to come and sing for us. You have a nice voice, and I think you could be a blessing to our people", he stalled again, and after three or four attempts he said, "Brother Strauss, I wish you had not asked me to come. You know, many of the people in the church you pastor come to me for treatment. You have three persons in your choir who over a couple of years have just added up a large sum of money. Two are schoolteachers with a regular income, and I do not want to embarrass them. They do not even make an effort to pay: their debt just keeps rising, and they never say a word about it. I would rather not embarrass them". I was embarrassed, I was ashamed. He did not tell me who they were, but when we gathered, and the choir sang, I said, "Lord, you know who they are, we need honesty in this church". There was a need for honesty. Am I totally honest with my spouse, with my children, with my parents, with my neighbours, with my business associates? Am I totally honest with my government? There is a need for honesty. Beloved, "My God shall supply all your need." You can't buy it with money!

Let us look at one more (verse 8). "Finally, brethren, whatsoever things are true, whatsoever things are honest, whatsoever things are just, (the word 'just' means right) whatsoever things are pure, whatsoever things are lovely, whatsoever things are of good report." That tells me there was a need for holiness in the church at Philippi. Do I practice holiness?

Not sinless perfection. "Be holy, for I the Lord am holy" God expects His people to be a holy people. Paul said, I am exhorting you. Notice it comes at the end: he said, Finally, before I close this letter, one final word: there is need for holiness. Then he ends the epistle with these words: "My God shall supply all your need". You can't buy holiness with money, no amount of money, you can't even work out holiness, holiness comes as a result of obedience to the Word of God.

Dear friends, this is one of the 'Alls' we have been talking about in this series: "My God shall supply all your need according to His riches in glory by Christ Jesus".

AMEN AND AMEN!

According to Your Faith

---------------------❖---------------------

'*According to your faith* ...' Matthew 9:29

One of the greatest chapters in the Bible is Hebrews 11. We know it best as *The Faith Chapter*. In its 40 verses the word 'faith' appears not less than twenty-five times.

The chapter commences with a definition of faith: "Now faith is the substance of things hoped for, the evidence of things not seen" (11:1). Faith is the ground, the basis, the confidence for things we cannot see. Faith that is seen is not faith at all (Romans 8:24, 2 Corinthians 4:18).

The chapter continues with a strong declaration of the indispensability of faith, for 'without faith it is impossible to please God' (1:6). God Himself must be the object of our faith, for He is pleased when He sees our faith in who

He is, and in the future He has planned for those who diligently seek Him.

There are several Scriptures which illustrate the fact that there are varying degrees of faith:

'No Faith' .... (Deut. 32:20; John 20:27)
'Little Faith' .... (Matt. 6:30; 8:26; 14:31; 16:8)
'Weak Faith' .... (Rom. 4:19-23)
'Strong Faith' .... (Rom. 4:19-23)
'Great Faith' .... (Matt. 8:10; Luke 7:9)
'Full of Faith' .... (Acts 6:5-8)
'Full Assurance of Faith' .... (Heb. 10:22)

How would you describe your faith? Before you attempt to answer this question remember, Jesus sees your faith (John 9: 12), and He knows your thoughts (John 9: 4). Be honest in your self-examination! Now test yourself.

Are you faithless, having no faith? Do you have little faith? Is your faith weak or is it strong? Do you have great faith? Are you full of faith? Do you have the full assurance of faith?

There is one way whereby we are able to increase our faith - "So faith cometh by hearing, and hearing by the Word of God" (Rom. 10: 17). The more we nourish our souls by feeding on the holy Scriptures, the stronger our faith will become. If faith is not nourished on the words of God, it becomes weak.

Faith cannot be fed on the things our eyes see. Beware of "the lust of the eyes" (1 John 2: 16). What we see with our eyes will tend to dim the truth of the holy Scriptures. Remember Eve (Gen. 3: 6)! Remember Achan (Josh. 7: 20,21)! Remember David (2 Samuel 11: 2-5)! And finally, remember Jesus and His reply to Satan (Matt. 4: 8-11)!

"Faith cometh by hearing, and hearing by the Word of God" (Rom. 10:17). Read our Lord's parable of the Sower, the Seed and the Soils. It appears in the Synoptic Gospels (Matt. 13; Mark 4: Luke 8). The Seed is the Word of God. The Soils are the different kinds of heart response to the Word. All four hearts heard the Word, but only one responded to the Word. In the first, the Devil stole the Word (Matt. 13: 19; Mark 4: 15; Luke 8: 12). In the second, the flesh starved the Word (Matt. 13: 20,21; Mark 4: 16,17; Luke 18: 13). In the third, the world strangled the Word (Matt. 13: 22; Mark 4: 18; Luke 8: 14).

"He that has ears to hear, let him hear" (Matt. 13:9; Mark 4: 23; Luke 8:8). But "Take heed how ye hear" (Luke 8: 18). And when you "hear the Word of God ... do it" (Luke 8: 21; John 2:5). "Faith cometh by hearing, and hearing by the Word of God."

The fourth heart in the parable received the Word, retained the Word and responded to the Word (Matt. 13: 23; Mark 4:20; Luke 8:15). As we follow this pattern daily, our faith will become stronger. "According to your faith be it unto you."

Sincerely in Christ,

LEHMAN STRAUSS